W9-BLP-348

BROTHERHOOD OF WARRIORS

Behind Enemy Lines
with a Commando
in One of the
World's Most Elite
Counterterrorism Units

BROTHERHOOD OF WARRIORS

AARON COHEN
AND DOUGLAS CENTURY

ecco
An Imprint of HarperCollins*Publishers*

This is a work of nonfiction: all the events depicted are true and the characters are real. Because several of the people depicted here are still active in the Israeli counterterrorism and intelligence communities, some personal and place names have been altered for privacy and security reasons. The names of certain terrorist targets also have been changed for privacy reasons and to avoid divulging confidential information that may endanger future missions and individuals. All dialogue has been re-created to the best of the author's recollection. The chronology of some events in Israel before my enlistment in the IDF has been streamlined.

HarperCollins books may be purchased for educational, business, or sales promotional use. For information, please write: Special Markets Department, HarperCollins Publishers, 10 East 53rd Street, New York, NY 10022.

FIRST EDITION

Designed by Susan Walsh

Library of Congress Cataloging-in-Publication Data is available upon request.

ISBN: 978-0-06-123615-0

08 09 10 11 12 ID/RRD 10 9 8 7 6 5 4 3 2 1

TO THE FALLEN WARRIORS

The basic difference between an ordinary man and a warrior is that a warrior takes everything as a challenge while an ordinary man takes everything as a blessing or a curse.

CARLOS CASTANEDA

BROTHERHOOD OF WARRIORS

The Dizengoff Massacre

Just after 4 P.M. on March 4, 1996, as Israel was busily preparing for the Purim holiday, a massive explosion tore through the heart of Tel Aviv.

I felt the blast before I heard it. Stretched out on Tal's sofa, I noticed the barrel of my machine gun vibrating. As the whole apartment house began to shake, a cheap alarm clock and a framed picture of Tal and two other Special Forces soldiers from our unit came crashing down from the shelf. I barely lifted my head from the sofa. Having grown up in Los Angeles, I'd long ago become accustomed to riding out earthquakes and their aftershocks.

Plus, I was too numb to move; my mind and body were fried. I was in Tel Aviv on my first overnight leave since joining the Special Forces a few months earlier. Somehow, I'd managed to make it through the brutal physical and psychological gauntlet to become a fully operational soldier—"warrior" or "fighter" is the literal translation from the Hebrew word *lochem*—and was eagerly awaiting my first undercover mission for Sayeret Duvdevan, Israel's elite Special Forces counterterrorism unit. Driving my Israel Defense Forces–issued car from our desert base to Tel Aviv, I wasn't thinking about Purim parties (in Israel the holiday is a time of drinking, feasting, and costumed mayhem in nightclubs). I wanted nothing more than a cold beer and a few hours' sleep on Tal's couch.

Tal was already in his third year in Sayeret Duvdevan. The name "Duvdevan" is something of an inside joke to Israelis; it literally means "cherry." As most Sabras (that is, native-born Israelis) know, there is a species of cherry in the Holy Land that looks no different from the edible variety but which packs a strong and often lethal poison. As a Special Forces unit operating undercover disguised as Palestinian men and women, Duvdevan is the "cherry" that may look harmless but often proves deadly. Tal was on his mandatory rotation out of the unit just as I was on my way in. A short, tautly muscled Sabra of Sephardic descent, he was arguably the unit's most talented counterterrorism instructor. He had the look and demeanor of the consummate *lochem*. His jet-black eyes rarely betrayed a glimmer of emotion; he never wasted a word, never bullshitted; and, like most Duvdevan vets, wouldn't regale the barracks with war stories of his past undercover missions in the *shetah*, Hebrew for "field." But in my first weeks of training, I'd heard it whispered that Tal's trigger finger had "neutralized" more Arab terrorists than cancer.

When the explosion hit, Tal was cracking open a couple of bottles of Maccabee lager; the beer foamed over and the shockwave jolted him against the refrigerator. He darted to his open balcony. I was close behind. The perfect Mediterranean blue sky was instantly darkening: a massive thunderhead of black smoke billowed down the street toward us.

"Piguah, piguah!" Tal yelled, Hebrew for terrorist attack. He was still completely calm, but his eyes darted back to the living room, locking on his machine gun.

I grabbed my own M-4, a lightweight version of the M-16, and we tore downstairs, heading in the direction of the Dizengoff Mall. If it was a terrorist bombing, I prayed the mall wasn't the target. Located at the intersection of Dizengoff and King George streets, it's the city's most popular shopping center, and on *erev* Purim, the intersection was sure to be packed with teenagers, tourists, schoolchildren, and young mothers with strollers. No more than half a minute after the explosion we arrived on the scene and my worst fears were realized: The bomb had ripped through an enormous section of wall, destroying the mall's entrance, leaving a scene of unspeakable carnage. Scores of mangled bodies and limbs were scattered everywhere: arms blown off, bodies decapitated. A female soldier stared up at me, howling and writhing, one leg missing below the hip, the other gashed beyond repair. I knew she'd likely bleed to death before we could set up triage. As I turned, my boot heel slipped on pavement slick with blood.

The Dizengoff Mall resembled a battlefield more than a crime scene. It didn't take Tal and me more than a few seconds to realize what we had to do: No one had a goddamn clue what was happening, and the collective sense of panic was escalating exponentially by the moment. All the usual authorities—the cops and the border patrol soldiers who park in front of the mall, checking bags—were dead or dying. Tal shot me a quick, fierce glance. I nodded, acknowledging that I understood it was now our duty to take charge of the crime scene.

Like all the elite commando units in the Israel Defense Forces (IDF), the fighters of the Sayeret Duvdevan carry two pieces of special identification. We have a card that says we're exempt from shaving, permission usually granted to ultra-Orthodox draftees who refuse to violate the biblical strictures against trimming their beard and side locks while in service, but in our case, issued solely to accommodate our need for disguise when we go undercover in the West Bank.

More important, we carry a "black clearance" pass which grants us the highest operational level of security clearance in the Israeli army. Members of the top-tier Special Forces units can go to any military base in the country, no questions asked, walk into classified recon rooms, even sit shoulder-to-shoulder with officers planning top-secret operations. The other thing black clearance allows us to do—actually requires us to do—is take charge of a scene of a terrorist attack, regardless of the ranking military or law enforcement officers present.

I chambered my M-4, began running through the mob, screaming in Hebrew, "Get the fuck out of the way! Move! *Move!*" I shouted at one girl who stared mutely back in terror. When she turned I saw the blood streaming down her face: There was a gaping, scarlet-and-black hole. Her eyeball had been blown clear out of the socket.

There are three basic rules of counterterror first response. *One*: spot all threats. *Second*: neutralize the threat. *Third*: sweep the area. Tal and I were looking for active threats: an unattended bag; an individual appearing too calm, staring ahead with tunnel vision; an individual screaming in a manic manner, especially shouting out words in Arabic. Having swept the area, and deemed it to be free of active threats, Tal and I began the gruesome work of dragging bodies to triage.

Then came a cacophony of horns as police cars and ambulances with sirens wailing raced to the scene of the massacre. Hearing sirens in Israel isn't like hearing them in any other Western country. In the United States, our first assumption might be that an old man keeled over with cardiac arrest, or some kid fell out of a tree, or a couple of Grand Ams or Camrys were in a fender bender on the freeway. But in Israel, the public is always on edge, always prepared for the worst-case scenario. The sound of sirens is often a harbinger of something catastrophic—usually, a massive loss of innocent civilian lives. And the Dizengoff Mall bombing attack was precisely that kind of catastrophe.

On a typical afternoon, the intersection of Dizengoff and King George streets is the most densely populated location in the whole State of Israel, a trendy hangout dotted by boutiques and chain stores like the Hard Rock Café, Benetton, and McDonald's. So many cars had been blown apart by the bomb, it was nearly impossible for first-response units to get access to the dead, mangled, and dying. But at last the ambulances and paramedics and cops began arriving. The desperate screaming and shrieking never seemed to subside. All around us, ultra-Orthodox volunteers from the Burial Society began the grisly job of gathering even the most minute fragments of human flesh and bone. It's next to impossible to convey the sense of utter chaos and carnage of that afternoon; we were literally slipping and falling in pools of blood.

No amount of training could have prepared me for the reality of that triage and rescue operation. My body simply did what it was supposed to do without waiting for orders from my brain. I went through the necessary motions physically, without taking the time to process the horrific images, although some realizations flashed through my mind before I could stop them.

That's a fragment of somebody's brain. That's a young woman's foot.

That Dizengoff Mall bombing changed me—my mentality, my focus, my commitment to my career in the IDF—forever. Working triage that awful Monday was the first time I ever had someone die in my arms.

She looked about fourteen, had braces on her teeth, and reminded me of my own kid sister, Adrienne, back in L.A. Her cheeks were streaked and smudged with bright red and yellow costume makeup; around her waist, badly tattered, I saw the remnants of charred reeds or grass, what must have been a Hawaiian hula girl's outfit. She kept asking me if she was going to die. I did my best to force a reassuring smile as I checked her pulse. She kept asking me, "Why?" as she was drifting away from me. I gave her mouth-to-mouth while Tal desperately pumped her chest, but within seconds, we both knew she was gone. I heard my own furious scream join the chorus of others.

And so it went until sunset. Just before six Prime Minister Shimon Peres arrived to survey the scene, surrounded by a thick security phalanx, all with weapons drawn. Tal and I barely noticed. We worked triage nonstop for four hours, until our vision was blurred and our fatigues were caked with dried blood. Around 8 P.M. our pagers went off. Tal grabbed my cell phone to contact the base.

"They're recalling the entire unit," he said.

"Holy shit," I said, "that's a lot of fighters." Israel's response would be swift, well coordinated, and merciless.

By now a senior police officer was on-site, attempting to organize the chaotic ad hoc triage into a systematic rescue operation. The cop tried to order us to stay but I raised my hands, indicating we had more pressing orders, telling him in Hebrew, "Sorry, we've been called back to our base." Tal was far more direct.

"Look, we're gone," Tal said, flipping the cop his black clearance ID card.

The cop nodded, understanding that a Special Forces retaliation mission would already have been ordered by the General Staff, and waved us on.

The Dizengoff Mall bombing marked the fourth major terrorist attack in nine days, a period of time that remains the worst, concentrated series of civilian massacres in modern Israeli history. The opening salvos came to be known, in chilling Hebrew shorthand, as the "Jerusalem 18" attacks. On the morning of February 25, 1996, a suicide bomber exploded on public bus Number 18 on the main Jaffa Road near the Jerusalem Central Bus Station. Twenty-six people were killed, and perhaps as many as eighty were injured. Less than thirty minutes later, a second suicide bomber blew up at a bus stop in the city of Ashkelon, killing two and wounding thirty-eight. Less than a week later, on the morning of March 3, 1996, another suicide bomber attacked the same Jerusalem 18 bus line, this time killing nineteen and wounding seven.

The bombings were determined by Shabak* to have been the work of Hamas.

The front-page headline in the March 5 *New York Times* would put the Dizengoff Mall attack, and indeed the entire weeklong terror campaign, into the context of the crumbling Oslo Peace Accords:

> **FOURTH TERROR BLAST IN ISRAEL**
> **KILLS 14 AT MALL IN TEL AVIV,**
> **NINE-DAY TOLL GROWS TO 61**
>
> The fourth in a series of suicide attacks in Israel struck in the heart of Tel Aviv, bringing the nine-day death toll to 61. Its own power threatened by public rage, the Government met in an emergency session and declared it was taking the all-out war against the new terrorism into areas under Palestinian control. . . . With the unforeseen wave of terror bombing and the stern Israeli response, the fate of Israeli-Palestinian accords [hangs] in the balance.†

For me, Dizengoff was *personal*. I was there amid the carnage, hands bloodied by the dying victims. Such was the devastation that the attack was initially thought to be the result of a massive car bomb. But the perpetrator was ultimately found to be a lone suicide bomber, a young, nervous Arab male carrying a twenty-kilogram bomb packed with nails. Detonated in a crowded urban environment, a nail bomb

---

* Israel's counterintelligence and internal security service, also known as Shin Bet. Shabak is the acronym of the agency's Hebrew name, Sherut ha-Bitachon ha-Klali.

† *New York Times*, March 5, 1996, by Serge Schemann.

is a primitive, barbaric, and hideously efficient weapon. All told, the Dizengoff suicide bombing resulted in thirteen dead and seventy-five injured, including two United States citizens.

An extremist response to the Oslo Peace Accords, the nine-day terror campaign by Hamas had Israel on the brink of widespread civil and political unrest. The Purim holiday slaughter marked the nadir in the entire peace process. In response to the terror wave, Israel had ordered that the borders to the Occupied Territories of the West Bank—referred to by religious Jews as "Judea and Samaria"—and the Gaza Strip be sealed. No Arabs were permitted to travel into Israel; every Jewish community in the territories was instructed to stop employing Arab day laborers.

There was a feeling of virtual anarchy in both the Israeli and the Palestinian communities, upheaval that can be fully understood only in light of the tremendous optimism that had greeted the signing of the Oslo Accords three years prior. Officially called the *Declaration of Principles on Interim Self-Government Arrangements*, the Oslo Accords called for the withdrawal of Israeli forces from parts of the Gaza Strip and West Bank—occupied by the Israeli military since its victory in the Six-Day War of 1967—and affirmed a Palestinian right of self-government within those areas through the creation of a Palestinian Authority. Palestinian rule would last for a five-year interim period during which a permanent agreement would be negotiated. Hot-button issues such as who would govern Jerusalem—the ancient city of David, sacred to Jews, Muslims, and Christians—the status of refugees, Israeli settlements in the area, security and borders were deliberately excluded from the Accords.

The negotiations were finalized in Oslo, Norway, on August 20, 1993, and officially signed at a public ceremony in Washington, D.C., on September 13, 1993, with Mahmoud Abbas, head of the Palestine Liberation Organization's Negotiations Affairs Department, signing for the PLO and Foreign Minister Shimon Peres signing for the State of Israel, witnessed by Warren Christopher for the United States and Andrei Kozyrev for Russia, in the presence of President Bill Clinton, Israel's Prime Minister Yitzhak Rabin with the PLO's Chairman Yasser Arafat.

Oslo was one of many attempts to broker lasting peace between Israel and its Arab neighbors. From the first peace conference in 1949, held on the island of Rhodes (formalizing an armistice in the 1948 War of Independence, which halted military hostilities between the newly founded Jewish state and the armies of Egypt, Jordan, Syria, and Lebanon), through the Camp David Accords of 1978 (at which U.S. president Jimmy Carter oversaw the historic handshake between Israeli prime minister Menachem Begin and Egyptian president Anwar Sadat, leading to the 1979 Israel-Egypt Peace Treaty), there were countless international efforts to find a lasting solution to the decades of bloodshed in the Middle East. However, what made the Oslo negotiations different was the decision to hold—for the first time—direct, face-to-face talks between Israel and Yasser Arafat's Palestine Liberation Organization, long deemed a terrorist group with too much blood on its hands to be included in any serious peace talks.

Following the collapse in 1991 of the Soviet Union—whose military had backed the Arab regimes in the Six-Day War of '67 and Yom Kippur War of '73—optimism among both the Israeli and American public was sky-high. It was a heady time. The historian Francis Fukuyama wrote an article in *National Interest* magazine, rhetorically asking if the world had now arrived at "The End of History?" Had the end of the Cold War heralded the beginning of a new international order? President George H. W. Bush seemed to believe that was the case and, ironically, on September 11, 1990, he spoke of a "rare opportunity" to move toward a "new world order" in which "the nations of the world, east and west, north and south, can prosper and live in harmony. . . . Today the new world is struggling to be born."

Israelis are, if nothing else, the ultimate pragmatists; and by the early 1990s they had tired of the ceaseless violence of the First Intifada, which had erupted near the end of 1987. Obviously the deep-seated roots lay in the then-twenty-year-long occupation of the West Bank and Gaza, but it's widely accepted now that the First Intifada sprang from a series of rumors and false allegations of Israeli atrocities and instigation from imams in various mosques. On December 6, 1987, a Jewish businessman was stabbed to death while shopping in Gaza. One day later, four residents of the Jabalya refugee camp in Gaza were killed in a traffic accident. Rumors quickly spread that the four had been killed by Israelis in a deliberate act of revenge for the stabbing of the Jewish businessman. Mass rioting broke out in Jabalya when a seventeen-year-old Palestinian, having thrown a Molotov cocktail at an army patrol, was shot dead by an Israeli soldier. Within hours, the mayhem had spiraled out of control, engulfing almost all the Arab communities of the West Bank, Gaza, and Jerusalem.

Soon there was widespread rock-throwing, barricaded roads, and flaming tires throughout the territories. By December 12, six Palestinians had died and thirty had been injured in the violence. The following day, rioters threw a gasoline bomb at the U.S. consulate in East Jerusalem; though no one was hurt, it was an ominous sign that the uprising was escalating to unprecedented levels. During the first four years of the uprising, according to Israel Defense Forces estimates, some 3,600 Molotov cocktail attacks, 100 hand grenade attacks, and 600 assaults with guns or explosives had been directed at soldiers and civilians alike. During this period, sixteen Israeli civilians and eleven soldiers were killed by Palestinians in the territories; more than 1,400 Israeli civilians and 1,700 Israeli soldiers were injured.

The First Intifada never officially ended, rather it petered into a state of bleak attrition. A growing sense of weariness about the daily bloodshed set in among both Jews and Arabs. The reign of terror became too much for the PLO; as more and more Palestinians expressed public concern about the disorder, Arafat's organization began to issue calls for an end to the Intifada, though the internecine murders continued. The Israeli historian Benny Morris has described the dire situation by the fourth year of the insurrection: "[T]he Intifada seemed to have lost direction. A symptom of the PLO's frustration was the great increase in the killing of suspected collaborators; in 1991 the Israelis killed fewer Palestinians—about 100—than the Palestinians did themselves—about 150."*

Meanwhile, during the First Gulf War (1990–1991), following Iraq's Invasion of Kuwait, the terrifying Scud-missile attacks on Israeli soil profoundly altered the Israeli sense of psychological security, making it clear that a supreme air force and superior technology were more important than holding territory (as a defensive buffer) in winning a military conflict.

---

* Benny Morris, *Righteous Victims: A History of the Zionist-Arab Conflict, 1881–1999*, Knopf, 1999.

As a result of these and other factors, most Israelis supported the Oslo Accords when they were first presented by Yitzhak Rabin's ruling Labor regime. With the successful signing of the Oslo Accords in the White House Rose Garden in September 1993, the Israeli government essentially recognized the PLO, and its political arm, Fatah, as the legitimate representative of the Palestinian people while the PLO recognized—a breakthrough of historic proportions—the right of the State of Israel to exist. It also renounced terrorism, violence, and its long-stated desire for the destruction of Israel.

The Oslo Accords aroused a surge of hope—yet skeptics abounded. Among Israeli politicians, the ruling left-wing Labor party, led by Rabin and Shimon Peres, strongly advocated the Accords, while the right-wing Likudniks, led by Benjamin "Bibi" Netanyahu, vehemently opposed them. After a two-day debate in the Knesset, Israel's parliament, a narrow vote of confidence was held on September 23, 1993, in which sixty-one Knesset members voted for the decision, fifty voted against, and eight abstained.

The Palestinian reaction to the Oslo Accords was not homogeneous, either. Arafat and his minions in Fatah accepted and advocated the Accords, but extremist groups such as the Palestinian Islamic Jihad, the Popular Front for the Liberation of Palestine, and especially Hamas, commonly known in Israel as the "refusal organizations," objected to the Accords since those groups loudly and violently denounced Israel's right to exist.

And, of course, both sides harbored fears of the other side's intentions. Israelis suspected that Arafat's faction was using the Oslo Accords as a tactic to buy time, that they were not sincerely trying to reach peace and coexistence with Israel but merely looking for a period of calm during which they could regroup and gather strength for a later armed conflict.

Since the start of the Second Intifada in September 2000—known as the "al-Aqsa Intifada" among the Arab camp, and "The Oslo War" among Jews who saw Israel making too many territorial concessions to the Palestinians—the Oslo Accords have been viewed with increasing disfavor by both the Palestinian and Israeli public. In May 2000, seven years after the Oslo Accords and five months before the start of the al-Aqsa Intifada, a survey by the Tami Steinmetz Center for Peace Research at the University of Tel Aviv found that 39 percent of all Israelis supported the Accords and that 32 percent believed that they would result in peace in the next few years. By contrast, the May 2004 survey found that 26 percent of all Israelis supported the Accords and 18 percent believed that they would result in peace in the next few years. Many Palestinians felt that the Oslo Accords had turned the PLO leadership into a tool of the Israeli state in suppressing their own people. While benefiting a small elite, the conditions of most Palestinians actually worsened. This was seen as one of the causes for the Second Intifada, the uprising in which I would spend the majority of my three-year stint with the IDF, serving on the front lines in those West Bank villages and cities roiling with hatred against the Israeli military occupation.

Within hours of the Dizengoff Mall massacre both Hamas and the Palestinian Islamic Jihad were scrambling to claim responsibility. The military wing of Hamas, the Izz ad-Din al-Qassam Brigades, released this statement to the media:

> Let the Jewish enemy know it is not safe from the strikes of our *mujahidin* despite the Nazi campaign it is launching against our innocent people. For neither organized killing, siege, starvation, nor house demolitions and sealing will frighten our *mujahidin*, who will, with God's will, keep fire on the necks of the Jewish terror leaders.

Tal and I were halfway through the Territories, en route to our top-secret Duvdevan base, when we heard the Hamas statement on the radio.

"Okay," I said, almost under my breath, "soon enough we're going to give it back to them." I let out a stream of guttural curses, mostly in Arabic—modern Hebrew having no decent swear words—then banged the steering wheel with the butt of my hand. Tal stared at me, eyes calm, sober, inscrutable as ever.

He was a seasoned warrior; he had already gone on countless undercover raids and operations in the West Bank. But this would be my first mission with Duvdevan. I was certain that many Special Forces and regular units of the IDF would be involved in retaliatory actions, but those of us in Sayeret Duvdevan would be engaging in some of the riskiest missions imaginable.

Founded in response to the upheaval of the First Intifada, the work of Duvdevan had become crucial to Israel's sense of national security. IDF Major-General Gabi Ofir once said that our unit was necessary to Israel's survival and, indeed, "the spearhead in the war against terror." When the First Intifada broke out in '87, the Israeli High Command was caught unprepared; the IDF initially tried to use traditional military tactics, resulting in abject failures. Instantly recognizable with their Uzis and M-16s, the Special Forces soldiers either found themselves in the middle of violent civilian riots, or when they finally arrived at a suspected terrorist's safe house, the target was long gone.

Thus, the need for brand-new *mista'aravim*, or "Arabist," counter-terrorism units, teams that could perform lightning-quick under-cover operations deep in the territories, arose again. The original *mista'aravim* squads of the 1940s, a tool of the early pre–State of Israel army, or Haganah, functioned primarily as intelligence-gathering units, dressing as Arabs to spy, run guns, and commit the occasional act of sabotage.

The new post-Intifada *mista'aravim* would be a different kind of fighting force entirely. In 1987, the IDF created two Special Forces *mista'aravim* units, dedicated specifically to counterterrorism missions in urban environments through undercover capability. Each was assigned a different area of operation. Sayeret Shimshon (or "Samson") was to operate in the Gaza Strip. Sayeret Duvdevan would operate in the West Bank. Although the two new entities were virtually identical in terms of training and expertise, the High Command chose to divide them into separate units since undercover work is as much art as it is science, and each Palestinian town, village, and region has its own distinct manners and customs with which the Special Forces operatives must be fully familiar.

In 1994, as a result of the Oslo Accords, the Gaza Strip was handed back to the Arabs, becoming an autonomous Palestinian Territory, which the Israel Defense Forces were not allowed to enter. Shimshon was disbanded, with many of its members being absorbed into Duvdevan and the remainder forming Egoz, an elite unit specializing in anti-guerrilla warfare assigned to the Golani Brigade in the Northern Command.

Duvdevan became the only *mista'aravim* counterterrorism unit active in the territories. And in the aftermath of the Dizengoff Mall massacre, it would fall primarily on us to undertake an immediate and lethal response. And unlike our enemies, we weren't going to spray shrapnel indiscriminately, targeting hundreds of innocent women and schoolkids. Nor would we abduct the low-level fanatics brainwashed into strapping on a nail bomb or a brick of C-4 in pursuit of glorious Islamic martyrdom. We'd be in pursuit of the behind-the-scenes architects, planners, and moneymen—paunchy, homicidal millionaires surrounded at all times by three or four bodyguards, the gray-bearded pseudo-intellectuals who could rationalize mass murder as a form of freedom fighting.

PART I

ONE

It began almost immediately after 9/11. My office in Beverly Hills was deluged with calls. Everyone, it seemed, from cable news producers to U.S. government officials, wanted the inside scoop on Israeli security methods. Could Israel's counterterrorism experts have prevented the hijackings? How do they profile potential suicide bombers? Train counterterrorist operatives? Rescue hostages?

On September 11, I was up before dawn—old military habits being impossible to break—and watched the attacks unfolding live on TV. *My God,* I said to myself. *It's finally happening here.* It had just been a matter of time before America was dragged into the jihad that Israel has been fighting for decades. One of the reasons that I returned to Los Angeles in 2000, after completing my three-year service in the Israel Defense Forces, was to pass on the cutting-edge counterterrorism techniques and sophisticated training I'd acquired as a counterterrorist commando in Israel. I knew that the United States was far too vulnerable to Islamic terrorist attacks and hoped I could do my part to sound the alarm before it was too late.

Ironically enough, though I've long considered Los Angeles my home, I wasn't even born in the United States, but in Montreal, Quebec, on February 28, 1976. My parents were part of the large English-speaking Jewish community that was soon to disperse to Toronto and other Canadian cities with the election of the Parti Québécois, which vowed to pursue "sovereignty" and separation from anglophone Canada.

My parents separated when I was small. I was constantly moving, never living in the same house for more than two years at a time. I spent the first decade of my life bouncing between homes in Montreal, Miami, and Los Angeles.

My mother's family was prominent in the Montreal Jewish community, my maternal grandfather having built up his trucking business into one of the largest in Canada. By the time my parents separated, my mother had developed a desire to leave Canada behind and pursue a career in the entertainment industry. In fact, she had already begun a fledgling career as a screenwriter and producer while still in Montreal. But she wanted a shot at the big league—success American style—and decided to relocate us to south Florida, where I had an aunt and uncle. My mother brought my sister and me down there temporarily, establishing a U.S. residency, until the divorce from my father was final. We lived together in Miami until I was about eight, at which point my mother decided to move again, this time to Beverly Hills. She told me offhandedly one day as she was dropping me off at elementary school that she simply couldn't take me with her to California. I would be staying behind to live alone with my aunt in south Florida. She needed to get her own life settled and would be taking my sister. Of course, I felt abandoned, but I did my best not to show any sense of hurt or frustration. I lived with my aunt and went to school on my own for the next year and pretty much stayed out of trouble.

Slowly, my mother's show-business career was taking off; by working hard and networking constantly, my mother was actually getting TV writing and producing gigs in Hollywood. It was while working on a film project in the late 1980s that she met the man with whom she would fall in love: Abby Mann, an older writer and producer who had won the 1961 Academy Award for Best Adapted Screenplay for the classic *Judgment at Nuremberg*. When they married in a small, private ceremony in L.A., he became my stepfather, taking my sister and me into his Beverly Hills home and raising us as his own children.

Los Angeles came as a shock. I'd seen the lavish lifestyle in movies and TV shows, but nothing could prepare me for the reality. Suddenly, my sister and I were walking into my stepfather's world, where brushing up against the biggest stars in the business was as commonplace as waving hello to the mailman. That first week in Beverly Hills, for example, Tony Bennett came over to the house; I spent an hour with his chauffeur riding around in our huge semicircular driveway in the first stretch limousine I'd ever set foot inside. Over the years, Frank Sinatra—and his various wives—would drop in for coffee and a chat. So would what was left of the Rat Pack: Dean Martin, Sammy Davis Jr., and old-time musicians like Buddy Rich. I quickly got a crash course in celebrity, learning that you had to put on an air of nonchalance, never seeming starstruck, even when you saw people like Warren Beatty, Steven Spielberg, Nicole Kidman, or Tom Cruise sitting in your living room talking over a script with your stepfather.

The money, especially the spending habits of the kids my age, was another matter entirely. I don't care how upper-middle-class you are by the standards of most places, the affluence of Beverly Hills is off the scale. Suddenly, I was surrounded by millionaires' kids, eight-year-olds growing up in palm-shaded palaces in the hills with Rolls-Royces in the driveway.

Life in Los Angeles wasn't such a big shock for my mother—her career was blossoming now, and she was making a name for herself as a film and television writer-producer. But to a kid my age, the adjustment was difficult, to say the least. It wasn't long before I started acting out in school—constantly being put on detention or called down to the principal's office for disrupting the class—and my mother acknowledged that the solution might be a more structured and traditional home environment. So while my sister stayed in Beverly Hills, I moved back in with my aunt's family in south Florida from ages eleven to twelve.

A year later, when the garage at their house in Beverly Hills was converted into a bedroom for me, I returned to Los Angeles, transferring to my fourth public school in as many years. You can imagine the disruption to my youthful psyche: changing cities, changing schools, constantly trying to make new friends and find a place to fit in. Adolescence is disorienting enough, let alone when you've been jumping around from city to city, and classroom to classroom. I learned to mask my uncertainties and insecurities by putting up an emotional wall, by acting as if nothing fazed me, and my mother and stepfather tried their best to create a sense of normalcy. But even something as All-American apple pie as Little League baseball can get downright surreal in Beverly Hills. Scott Caan, the son of James Caan, was one of my teammates on the Pirates in 1984 and 1985. We all liked Scotty, but we *loved* Jimmy, who was one of our coaches.

Jimmy would show up on his Harley with some gorgeous young woman on the back, and there was always a different girl for every game. He obviously hadn't slept and was still bombed from the night before. Jimmy was passionate about baseball. He actually wanted Scott to turn professional. But Scott wanted to be an actor instead.

Jimmy would show up at the ballpark, blasted out of his mind, and start yelling and flipping out at the umpires for making a bad call. I was still pretty new to L.A. and seeing such over-the-top movie-star antics was a little scary. That's what it was like growing up in Beverly Hills: You've got Tony Bennett's limousine circling in your driveway; you've got Frank Sinatra asking your mother for a warm-up on the coffee; you're playing Little League ball, and there's Sonny Corleone in wraparound shades, running out of the stands to kick dirt on the umpire for calling your ass out at first base.

Most of my newfound friends were little brats who'd grown up around all this affluence, privilege, and pretense. They were the kids of the stars, the producers, the studio executives, the *Variety* columnists, the agents like Rowland Perkins, Jim Wyatt, Jeff Berg, Nancy Josephson—all the heavy hitters who were known for making and breaking careers in that town. It was an elite club; we felt like L.A. royalty. The downside was that we were completely disconnected from any sense of family, or community, or values because our parents were so into themselves and their careers. They gave us money and toys to go play, and it seemed to me that the more money your family had, the more fucked up you were likely to be. My relationship with my stepfather was cordial, at best. He always seemed to have a cocktail in one hand and a script in the other. He'd never asked about my homework, my sports teams, or my friends, and throughout those early years, treated me like a piece of furniture that had been moved into his house with only his grudging consent. Weeks would go by when we never exchanged a word. Luckily, I had my sister, otherwise I think the loneliness and tension in that house would have been unbearable.

Like a lot of my friends in Beverly Hills, I had only the most superficial connection to Judaism. I'd been going through the motions in synagogue on the High Holy Days, but I knew next to nothing about either the culture or the religion, and certainly had no deep understanding about the history of the State of Israel.

Back when I was twelve years old, in fact, I wanted to become bar mitzvah, but my mother was too wrapped up with one of her screen projects to actually plan a proper bar mitzvah for me. So I asked my mother if I could live with my father for the year. She agreed, knowing that my father would view it as his paternal obligation to make a bar mitzvah of me. I lived in Montreal with my dad for that one year in sixth grade and it was one of the best years of my life. I got into some minor-league trouble in Canada and my father played the no-bullshit disciplinarian. After a year, I came back to L.A. and that's when my wildness started in earnest. If my tough-as-nails father in Montreal could barely control me, my mother in Beverly Hills had no prayer.

By seventh grade, I was attending Beverly Hills Middle School, one of four schools that feed into Beverly Hills High. As soon as

I started acting out in school again the educational psychologists were brought on board. They diagnosed me as having problems with authority, perhaps attenion deficit disorder—whatever educational jargon they used, I had it. What it came down to was I wanted to do things I liked and I wouldn't do what the teachers or my parents told me. I'd sit there in school, bored out of my skull, thinking: *How the fuck do you expect me to sit here and learn? It's Southern California and there are a thousand and one distractions out there.*

There was a lot of drug use at school, and not just bathroom toking. We had seventh-graders tripping on acid and other psychedelics. I had enough sense to stay away from the hard drug scene, but I was crying out for attention—positive, negative, any kind at all—from my parents. So when I was fourteen, I stole my parents' car, and swiped their credit cards. Sure enough, that got me some attention. It also got me sent away to military school. Technically, I didn't *steal* the car. My folks were out of town for a month shooting a movie, and I started driving their BMW 700-series to school every day. Two years before I could legally get a driver's license, I'm racing around L.A in a brand-new Beemer, profiling with my buddies, driving everybody to the mall and the burger joints. When my parents found out, they were furious, but it got even worse when those credit card bills showed up in the mailbox. Ironically, though, I hadn't been trying to do anything sneaky. I wanted to get caught.

My mom and I were on vacation in Miami, staying at my aunt's place, when the shit hit the fan. In one billing cycle, I'd put about ten grand on the credit cards.

"Aaron!" my mother sputtered, her face turning bright red. "Do you know anything about these charges? You've been using my Visa again?"

I just shrugged. I had my emotional wall well constructed by now.

"That's it. I give up. You're going to military school."

"Fine," I said, looking down at the brick pattern in the kitchen linoleum. "I don't give a shit."

"When we get back to L.A., start packing for Canada," she said. "You're starting next semester at Land."

About ten years earlier, my cousin Mark had been a troublemaker himself, and had been sent, against his will, to an infamous military school in Ontario known as the Robert Land Academy.

The thought of military school would have freaked out most guys. But for me it was actually a relief. Deep down I knew I needed some structure, some priorities, and most important, some discipline in my life. I'd bounced around so much by that point—Montreal, Miami, Los Angeles—I'd sometimes wake up in the morning and not remember what city and country I was in, or what school I was supposed to go to for first-period class.

It shouldn't have been a big surprise to anyone: all the moving around, all the emotional disruption and the isolation. It had been hard to form long-lasting friendships. I felt like I'd practically raised myself. By the time I was fourteen, I'd shuttled between the homes and schools in Canada, Florida, and California, back and forth, about half a dozen times.

I was desperately looking for some structure, a formalized sense of having a place in the world. In my aunt's house in Miami, my mother thought she was punishing me with her finger-wagging "Aaron, you're going away to military school" bullshit, but secretly, I was doing fucking somersaults.

TWO

I arrived at the Robert Land Academy, a sprawling, sixty-eight-acre campus located in the Niagara Peninsula, about a ninety-minute drive south of Toronto, during Christmas break of ninth grade, just before the second semester kicked off.

You couldn't paint a more stark contrast to the laxness, entitlement, and apathy I'd become accustomed to at Beverly Hills Middle School. Robert Land was steeped in tradition and a sense of history. Everything was by the military rulebook. If you got caught swearing, you would be ordered to chew a bar of soap. If you didn't complete a math assignment, there was no detention, no stern talking-to; they tied a twenty-pound weight jacket to your ass and made you run around the fucking lap track until you felt like you were going to puke.

The discipline was so hardcore when I was there in the early nineties, that they have since had to tone down a lot of the things that are now deemed illegal, like chewing soap or being forced to dig ditches in the freezing rain for getting a D in algebra class. Yet the academy could also be surprisingly progressive, for example, by allowing the boys themselves to run the school. There was a chain of command—all the boys have ranks such as lance corporal, corporal, and sergeant—and most of the marching drills and room inspections were conducted by the higher-ranking boys from the older grades. It's an integral part of the educational experience: instilling discipline by granting responsibility and accountability.

Rather than rebel against the discipline, I came into my own. It took a few months' adjustment, of course, but by my second and third semesters at Land, I found myself thriving in this military environment. Once I was given the structure and attention I needed, my natural inclination to succeed emerged. The teachers could see it, too. During my second year, I was invited to join the Young Leadership Program. After excelling there, I was promoted to Lance Corporal Cohen and given a platoon to command. It was my job to get them marching in formation in the morning, to inspect their beds, and make sure all their kit was in order. This was the first position of responsibility and leadership that I'd ever had.

It was during this time that I first became obsessed with the Israeli military. The headmaster of the school was an officer in the Royal Canadian Army, Colonel Scott Bowman. He was a Canadian intelligence officer who had done a yearlong stint in Israel, working with an international peacekeeping delegation around the time of the Yom Kippur War in the 1970s. Bowman was always immaculately dressed in his dark blue uniform, and he had the kind of penetrating gaze a young kid is afraid to look directly into. He had a degree in philosophy and a master's in educational consulting and he was extremely well read in literature, history, and military theory. He had plenty of theories about how to get to the core disciplinary problems of troubled kids. And to us—the troubled kids, pimply and gangly and impressionable—though he stood only about five foot nine, Colonel Scott Bowman was truly larger than life.

The First Gulf War, or "Operation Desert Storm," broke out in 1990 while I was at the Robert Land Academy. Colonel Bowman would bring in detailed maps of the Middle East and set them up on easels at lunchtime. I watched in silence, bordering on awe, as Bowman explained the ground war from a trained military officer's perspective, breaking down complicated strategies into building blocks a fourteen-year-old could comprehend, discussing details like how a fast-racing armored division couldn't afford to outrun its supply lines, just as Napoleon had famously said that an "army travels on its stomach."

And from time to time during these military strategy sessions, Colonel Bowman would talk about the Israeli military. He told us that the Israelis were—bar none—the most elite, cutting-edge military in the world. The first day Bowman talked about his time in Israel, I noticed a set of small, shiny silver wings on his lapel. Months later, I learned that these were highly coveted Israeli paratrooper jump wings and that they meant that Colonel Bowman had risked his own neck, on more than one occasion, plummeting five thousand feet into the Negev Desert while completing the esteemed course at Israel's Parachuting Jump School. For the first time in my life I was exposed to real-world role models, men whose achievements

I badly wanted to model my future on. The Robert Land Academy completely rewired me and Colonel Bowman played a huge part in my transformation. To this day, I associate Bowman's integrity, self-assuredness, and discipline with his Israeli training. And while I never mustered the courage to ask Bowman specifics—he wasn't approachable to any of us that way—I absorbed everything he had to offer. Over and over, he said that the Israelis were the toughest, smartest soldiers, and it was the greatest privilege of his military life to work with them. He admired their capabilities as soldiers, their values, and the totality of the commitment to self-defense that the State of Israel represented. He'd come to admire Israeli culture as a whole, especially the way the country came together in times of crisis, as it most famously did during the Six-Day War of 1967, when, threatened with annihilation by Arab enemies on all sides, the nation rallied not just to defend its borders but to achieve an unprecedented conquest of land held by the Egyptians, Jordanians, and Syrians.

When I actually moved to Israel five years later, I realized that Colonel Bowman was talking less about the infinitely more complex and fractious Israeli society of today and more about the original Zionist-socialist founders, the old-school Israelis who established the country after the Holocaust.

Though not Jewish himself, Colonel Bowman was particularly sensitive to the needs of the Jewish students at the academy. There were only four of us and Bowman always arranged for us to attend High Holy Day services at a synagogue in nearby Hamilton, Ontario.

I was the only one of the Jewish kids who became fascinated—to the point of obsession—with Colonel Bowman's remarks about the Israeli military. I started scouring the school library, pulling every book I could find on the Israel Defense Forces or the history of the State of Israel. I studied the War of Independence—or first Arab-Israeli War—when, the moment David Ben-Gurion publicly announced the establishment of the State of Israel on May 14, 1948, the new Jewish nation was attacked on all sides by the massed Arab armies. I studied the Six-Day War of 1967, when the pan-Arabist President Nasser of Egypt thought he could rally the Arab states to "drive the Jews into the sea." Instead, Israeli generals like Moshe Dayan captured the West Bank from Jordan and the Gaza Strip and Sinai Peninsula from Egypt. I pored over accounts of the Yom Kippur War of 1973, when a sneak attack by Egyptian and Syrian forces led to Israel's occupation of the Golan Heights in the north. But the most mesmerizing stories of all involved Israeli Special Forces missions, especially the legendary Raid on Entebbe in July 1976, when a handful of elite Israeli commandos flew a daring midnight mission into Uganda, rescuing more than one hundred hostages—innocent civilians who'd been taken captive by Palestinian terrorists on a hijacked Air France jet—right from under the murderous dictator Idi Amin's nose.

I read for hours and hours, until my eyes were bleary, like some kind of young Talmudic scholar, studying the names of the elite units—Sayeret Matkal, the oldest and most prestigious Special Forces unit that had achieved the historic success at Entebbe; Sayeret Shaldag, the Israeli Air Force's S.F. unit; and Shayetet-13 (or "Flotilla-13"), equivalent to the U.S. Navy SEALs. I read *The Elite* by Samuel M. Katz, and then went on to finish his entire series on the IDF. I read famous essays written by the legendary commanders of the IDF, men like Yitzhak Rabin, Ehud Barak, Shimon Peres, and Ariel Sharon.

I learned that even before the State of Israel existed, as the threat of a Nazi occupation of the Holy Land loomed, the Haganah, the paramilitary group that formed the core of the later Israel Defense Forces, formed an elite corps called Palmach—an acronym for *Plugot Mahatz*, which translates as "Strike Companies." The Palmach was the earliest incarnation of the Israeli Special Forces and many later generals and prime ministers such as Moshe Dayan, Yitzhak Sadeh, Yigal Allon, and Yitzhak Rabin were Palmach veterans. They had undeniable swagger but a complete lack of traditional military decorum, wearing baggy khaki shorts with their shirts wide open at the neck, and they didn't insist on protocol, insignia, or saluting. Superior officers were even addressed by their Hebrew nicknames.

As I pored over the military histories and studied the photos of the elite units from the Palmach through Matkal, what leapt out at me most was the lack of pomp and circumstance. The men's uniforms were rumpled, their hair disheveled, faces sunburned, unwashed, unshaven. It was the antithesis of everything I was learning at that military school—the spit and polish, the attention to sartorial detail. According to Colonel Bowman, *these* were the world's greatest warriors? For months, I was trying to make sense of the disconnect. How could my headmaster, who was so well groomed and Scots-Canadian handsome, with never so much as one hair out of place, have so much respect for a bunch of guys that looked so *slovenly*?

It wasn't until I got to Israel years later that I put the jigsaw pieces together: Like Moshe Dayan, Yitzhak Sadeh, and the old-school Palmach commanders, Israeli fighters didn't give a damn about pristine images. They were about the *feeling*, depth of commitment, and getting the mission done. Those Israelis weren't worried about looking polished and immaculate for the parade. But when it came to undertaking dangerous missions, as Colonel Bowman constantly said, there wasn't a fighting force on earth to match them.

> Meir Har-Zion was not a sociable man. He was not made for lavish receptions, or good public relations. He was a true fighter, the greatest fighter we have ever had. His activities, spread over a relatively short period, left a strong impact on the IDF and its soldiers for many years—for generations.
>
> —Ariel Sharon, former Israeli prime minister

The more I studied, the more intensely those pioneering warrior-kibbutzniks—collective farmers-turned-soldiers in times of national crisis—became my boyhood idols, my own version of the biblical heroes like King David, Joseph, and Elijah the Prophet whom I'd studied during the training for my bar mitzvah. I learned the names of each era's towering legends. Names like Joseph Trumpeldor, Alexander Zeid, Chaim Shturman, Orde Wingate, Hannah Senesh, Zvi Brenner, Gur Meirov, Itzhak "Gulliver" Ben-Menachem, Yoni Netanyahu, Ehud Barak. Some of the books related stories of shocking brutality, like the accounts of the missions of Unit 101—the first Special Forces outfit in the modern State of Israel—patterned after the British SAS,* which existed for only two years. In August

---

* The Special Air Service Regiment (SAS) is the principal Special Forces unit of the British Army, often credited with being the pioneering Special Forces unit anywhere and still regarded as among the most elite fighting forces in the world. The SAS can trace its existence back to 1941, when British army volunteers conducted raids behind enemy lines in the North African Campaign of World War II. The regiment's motto is *Who Dares Wins*.

1953, the nascent Israel Defense Forces formed a dedicated S.F. unit, dubbed "Unit 101," designed to perform complex reconnaissance and retaliatory missions beyond Israel's borders. Those behind-enemy-lines missions, undertaken primarily under Ariel Sharon's personal command, became known as the era of Reprisal Raids. The 1950s were something of the "Wild West era" between Israel and its warring Arab neighbors, and the missions of Unit 101 were—and remain to this day—immensely controversial. Arab terrorists—then largely referred to as *fedayeen*—would regularly slaughter Jews on Israeli soil; Unit 101 would counterstrike in enemy territory with no goal other than exacting a heavy price in terms of Arab lives and fear of future reprisals. By modern-day standards, Unit 101 was a minuscule outfit, composed of twenty to twenty-five soldiers honing tactics that formed the basis for all future Israeli Special Forces: stealth, small-unit maneuvers, and lightning-quick strikes at enemy strongholds and high-priority targets. Unit 101 created an international furor after a raid in which it was accused of killing as many as seventy unarmed civilians in the West Bank village of Qibya in October 1953. The U.S. State Department, formally denouncing the raid, demanded that those responsible for the slaughter be "brought to account." This forced the Israeli political leadership to forbid the IDF from directly targeting civilians in the future. Unit 101 continued to run missions, primarily against Arab military targets, until it was officially disbanded in 1955.

Curled up in the Robert Land library, reading accounts of the earliest Special Forces missions, a single name leapt out at me as a giant among giants. Meir Har-Zion was a dour, tough-as-nails warrior, who had been wounded during a reprisal raid on an Arab police station inside Jordan. He defined the era. He was more than a highly innovative and charismatic soldier; he was always the first man over the hill, the first man to storm through the door. (In Israel today, it's commonplace to hear soldiers joking about how U.S. and British commanding officers tend to stay "in the rear with the gear," while in Israel, officers like Har-Zion, and later, Yoni Netanyahu, literally lead the way forward into the firefight.) I recall reading an essay, titled "The Best Fighter We Ever Had," in which the future Prime Minister Ariel Sharon described Har-Zion's impact:

> There are fighters who shine in one battle. There are legendary commanders who have excelled in one war. Meir Har-Zion is a fighter and a commander of an era. From 1953 to 1956 he fought as a soldier and an officer, leading scores of operations, from which he returned only after they were successfully completed. A single Jordanian bullet ended his activity during that period.
>
> That night in September 1956, we rushed to the hospital in Beersheva after having captured and totally destroyed the Jordanian police fortress at A-Rahawa on the Beesheva-Hebron Road. Our action had been the reprisal for the murder of Jews by Palestinian terrorists. I remember the worried face of Chief of Staff Moshe Dayan, who must have also noticed a similar expression on my face. We were waiting for the doctor's report on Meir's condition. He had been wounded badly in the neck and only immediate medical care on the battlefield had saved him.
>
> The bullet had hit Meir when, as usual, he was leading the fighters in breaking through the gate and attacking the Jordanian fortress. That same night, in the corridor of the hospital, anxious

about Har-Zion, who was twenty-two at the time, I again thought about the high price that we were paying in dead and wounded in this endless battle against the Palestinian terrorists.*

Reading the stories of legendary warriors like Meir Har-Zion already had whetted my appetite. But I was only vaguely planning on traveling to Israel until I met the little general. By the time I finished my second year at Robert Land I had really come into my own. I wasn't even seventeen yet, but I was the fourth-highest-ranking cadet in the academy. I was thriving, and I would have stayed through graduation, but my mother—being in many respects a typically doting, protective, sentimental Jewish mother—deeply regretted all the time we'd spent apart during my rocky adolescence and her nascent career and new marriage. Perhaps, too, she'd seen the change in me, sensed the newfound maturity, and figured I could finally handle the extravagance and temptation of life in Beverly Hills.

"It's enough already," she said to me once, during a long-distance call. "Enough with the military school. Come home, Aaron. I'd love to see you every morning for breakfast."

So we agreed. I would spend my senior year at Beverly Hills High School. Plus, the Ontario school system has a Grade 13, so I would have had to complete two more years before graduating from the Robert Land Academy, whereas I'd only have to finish one more year back in Beverly Hills. At home that summer, I felt like a typical

---

* "The Best Fighter We Ever Had: Meir Har-Zion," by Ariel Sharon, in *Lionhearts: Heroes of Israel* (ed. Michael Bar-Zohar), New York, Warner Books: 1998.

seventeen-year-old: I was into girls, sports, heavy metal bands, fast cars, and motorcycles.

One day, after I'd been hanging out with my friends at the Beverly Center Mall, I came home and saw a short, squat little man in our backyard on Whittier Drive talking calmly and deliberately to my stepfather. He had snow white hair, piercing blue eyes, and sunburned forearms. His shirt was open, revealing his curly white chest hairs. I noticed he was enunciating so carefully because my stepfather had set up a professional microphone in order to tape-record their entire conversation by the pool.

As it turned out, my stepfather was working on a project for HBO about the racist skinhead subculture in Europe and he was interviewing this high-ranking general in the IDF about what the Israeli intelligence community knew about the rising tide of neo-Nazis in Europe.

"Oh, here's Aaron now," my stepfather said, calling me out to the pool to introduce us. Abby had obviously been talking to the general about me. This was typical: my stepfather only seemed to notice me, showing me off like a trophy, when he had some visitor at the house he was trying to impress.

"I heard you did well at this military school," the general said.

I nodded, told him the impressions I'd formed about the Israeli army from Colonel Bowman and from my extensive reading.

I had no *clue* at the time what a high-level officer I was talking to. A commanding officer of the paratroopers division, he was a highly decorated career soldier who'd fought in every war since the founding of the State of Israel. For some reason—probably because I'd just come home from military school—the general took an instant liking to me. He pulled me into a half bear hug. I'll never forget the weight of his muscular arm on my shoulder, his conspiratorial baritone, the smell of martini olives on his breath. I was trying my best not to look overexcited, but I couldn't believe my good fortune; here I had the chance to sit poolside and pick the brain of a general from the legendary paratroopers division.

The general was plain-spoken, blunt in that uniquely Israeli way. "Look, Aaron," he said, cutting right to the chase, "it's one thing to hear all these *stories* about Israel. It's one thing to read *books* about Israel, you know? But why don't you actually *go* to Israel?"

I was silent for a long time, listening to the wind rustling through the nearby palms. "I was thinking about doing that," I said, though, in reality, the seed that had been planted by Colonel Bowman had not yet begun to sprout an actual, feasible plan.

The general gave me a serious once-over, analyzing me in a millisecond, seeing what I was made of. "You seem like a strong guy. You keep yourself fit. Israel is always looking for good people, especially strong Jewish boys like you. Listen, you should go to Israel and check it out."

Imagine the impact on me: This was the first real Israeli soldier—let alone officer—I'd ever talked to. I was blown away by how soft-spoken and commanding he was. Burning with curiosity, I pushed him for details, but he wouldn't talk about his career. He shrugged; he sighed; he shut down completely. It was something I would later come to know well in Israel, a hardened warrior mentality—making no commitments, no promises, no formal advice.

"Look, just go there with an open mind," he said. "And, Aaron, when you get there—listen to me now—don't be a big shot, okay?" Israelis are constantly telling you that: *Don't be a big shot.* "Go there and be nice and quiet. See what's going on. See what's cooking.

And, if you like the smell of the food, okay, so then you go into the kitchen."

I laughed aloud. The little general had a way with words. "If you like what's cooking in the kitchen, *then* you sit down and have a meal."

I glanced at my mother and my stepfather. Like most upper-middle-class Jews, my parents had always expected me to get a university education. But after talking to the general for a few hours, a college degree seemed pointless. My higher education would be found in Israel.

By the time I sat down for my first class at Beverly Hills High, I'd found my ambition: to make aliyah to Israel, become a citizen, and do my three years of military service. And I had an even loftier goal, one I didn't dare speak out loud: to become not just a regular soldier in the Israel Defense Forces but a commando in one of the Tier One all-volunteer Special Forces units.

The word *aliyah* literally means "ascent" or "going up" in Hebrew. In the synagogue, an aliyah means being called before the Holy Ark to read from the Torah, which is what a thirteen-year-old does on his bar mitzvah day. In Zionist terms, though, making aliyah is a fundamental concept enshrined in the Law of Return, the cornerstone of Zionist philosophy which permits any Jew the legal right of immigration and settlement in Israel, as well as automatic Israeli citizenship. In 1950, the Knesset passed a simple but remarkable law which came to define Israel's central purpose as a nation-state.

Every Jew has the right to immigrate to this country.

Two thousand years of the Diaspora, of wandering, were officially over. In essence, this meant that all Jews worldwide, no matter their country of origin, are Israeli citizens by right. In 1955, the law was amended slightly to specify that dangerous criminals could be denied their right under the Law of Return. In 1970, the Knesset took a further historic step by granting automatic citizenship not only to Jews but to their non-Jewish children, grandchildren, and spouses, and to the non-Jewish spouses of their children and grandchildren. This addition not only ensured that families would not be broken apart but also promised a safe haven in Israel for non-Jews subject to persecution because of their Jewish roots.

It sounds simple in theory. But as with everything involving immigration and government bureaucracy, there's a truckload of paperwork to deal with just to make aliyah. The first step was going down to the Jewish Agency in Los Angeles for an interview. The most important thing they stressed was that I start learning Hebrew. I signed up to be part of the Ulpan* program, to travel to a kibbutz in the north of Israel, which would serve as my formal "absorption center" and where I would immerse myself in the language and culture. I also started dropping by an international newsstand to buy Hebrew-language newspapers, and listening to countless hours of Hebrew audiotapes.

That spring, I was well on my way to completing all the necessary paperwork, arranging my visas, and making sure my aliyah pro-

* Ulpan, meaning "studio" or "instruction," is an institute for the intensive study of Hebrew, specifically designed to teach adult immigrants to Israel the basic skills needed for conversation, writing, and comprehension and thereby more quickly integrate into mainstream Israeli society. Most *ulpanim* also provide instruction in the fundamentals of Israeli culture, history, and geography.

cess went off without a hitch when I was called, unexpectedly, one morning into the principal's office. The secretary was visibly upset.

"Aaron," she said, "your mother is on the phone. And we are *really* sorry."

"Sorry about what?"

"We're so, so sorry."

I grabbed the phone and my mother was talking a mile a minute. "They did it. They really *did* it! They burned the house down!"

I didn't need her to explain any more; I knew what had happened. My mother and stepfather had been making a movie about a controversial criminal investigation for a major TV network. There had been several threats leading up to this attack, and while it was ruled an act of arson, the police have never officially solved the case.

I was let out of school and my mom and my stepdad came to pick me up. They were understandably devastated. But, strangely, I felt like I was outside of the scene, watching it happen to *another* Aaron, *another* family.

My mother kept saying how sorry she was about all my records, my drum kit, my sports equipment, my pictures and posters—everything we lost in my bedroom. But even at the age of seventeen, I had very few material attachments. I suppose it had to do, in part, with having moved around so much since I was a toddler. I'd learned not to get too attached to anything physical. But it also had to do with my intense focus on making aliyah. For the first time in my life, I had a concrete goal, a sense of purpose that deepened with every day.

We moved, temporarily, into the Bel Age Hotel on North San Vicente Boulevard in West Hollywood. My parents took a suite. I had a room on the same hall, just a few doors down. Sounds luxurious, I know, and it was a trendy place with movie stars and other assorted celebrities traipsing in and out, but by Beverly Hills standards, it was nothing too debauched. No sand dunes of blow on my glass coffee table, no orgies or hookers passed out in the bathtub.

I kept my tunnel vision on making aliyah to the Holy Land. I was no longer the wild child I'd been at fourteen. I was single-minded now, keyed in on two things: training my body to be fit for my army call-up, and learning rudimentary Hebrew in order not to be such a fish out of water when I landed in Tel Aviv.

Up every day at the crack of dawn, I was pumping weights at six A.M., doing push-ups and calisthenics, running three miles a day. The football field at Beverly Hills High rivals many college stadiums: Astroturf, spanking-new scoreboard, a miniature Rose Bowl. I'd be out there all the time, running on the track, pushing myself harder than most of the varsity athletes. Every coach at the school was trying to recruit me—football, baseball, track and field. But I told them all I wasn't interested.

"Sorry, I'm not doing it for Beverly. I'm doing it for my own reasons."

"What kind of reasons, Cohen?"

"I'm going to Israel to work on a kibbutz and then I'm going to join the Army."

I knew that as soon as I graduated, I would be on that jumbo jet to Israel. Nothing could distract me. Some nights I'd leave my buddies alone to party with girls in my room at the Bel Age; meanwhile, I was down at the Jewish Community Center, taking night classes in modern Hebrew.

THREE

My last day in Los Angeles was more stressful than I'd imagined. My mother wasn't taking my imminent departure too well. I could see it in her eyes. I wasn't flying to Israel on some short-term tourist visa; nor was this the typical scene of an eighteen-year-old going away for freshman year of college. Far more than sadness, my mother's face was filled with fear. We didn't talk about it openly, but she knew I had bought a one-way ticket to Tel Aviv and I wasn't coming back until I accomplished what I'd set out to accomplish.

She'd accepted it, even given me her perfunctory blessing. But now the reality was sinking in that a stint in the Israeli army is a minimum of three years.

She was silent during the drive to the airport, sniffling, dabbing the corners of her eyes with a Kleenex, looking out the window so

I wouldn't see her crying. I kept glancing over at her as I drove her car. She was trying to let me go, I realized. But it wasn't going to be easy on either of us.

When we said our good-byes in the LAX terminal she looked like she was going to have a nervous breakdown, sobbing loudly and hugging me like it was the last time we'd ever lay eyes on each other. I'd never seen my mother so emotional about anything. But I was no longer her baby boy and we both understood that when I returned from Israel I was going to be a changed man, hardened and altered in ways neither one of us could imagine. The next time she saw me, I would be an Israeli.

I wiped away her tears with Kleenex, but I couldn't allow myself to get sentimental. With a final kiss, I turned away, threw my duffel bag on my shoulder, and got on the plane.

One of the best things about making aliyah is that the Israeli government covers your expenses. My flight was paid for and a week before my departure, I'd shipped to Israel a crate containing my pride and joy: a brand-new, candy-apple red Suzuki RF600, hoping the motorcycle would arrive in the first few weeks after I got settled on the kibbutz. I was flying with the bare minimum, just my cell phone, a few basic Hebrew books, and a duffel bag of clothes. My activities on the kibbutz were deemed volunteer work, and the army pay I would be receiving was next to nothing. My parents were supportive of me, but not quite so enthusiastic that they intended to bankroll me with a lavish parental stipend, so I was going to have to live in Israel as frugally as possible.

A nonstop flight from LAX to Tel Aviv's Ben-Gurion Airport lasts more than twelve hours. For many Jews, a flight to the Holy Land is a unique and supremely moving experience. My plane happened to be packed with Israelis who'd been traveling in India, the Himalayas, Bali, Thailand—and for them, it was nothing more than a routine flight home. But for many of the foreign-born Jews on the plane like me, the journey to Israel carried profound emotional meaning.

All around me, I noticed people reading from small Hebrew prayer books. Tiny copies of *Tehillim*, the Psalms of King David, were especially popular. The religious Jews on the flight got up several times to make a *minyan*—a group of ten men who are bar mitzvah—to pray together, pulling their *tallitot* (prayer shawls) over their shoulders and heads, davening in their hypnotically swaying style.

Apart from the ultra-Orthodox passengers, there was a distinctive, secular vibe on the plane, which meant we were in a permanent state of semi-chaos. Israelis are extremely impatient as a rule—they hate waiting their turn in line, and they have no patience for etiquette, politeness, or decorum. I watched in amazement as all these people, who couldn't be bothered to wait for the flight attendant to come their way, jumped up, roamed around the galley, and helped themselves to cans of Cokes, apple juice, and bags of chips.

I kept quiet, reading my Hebrew instructional books, until I decided to practice my Hebrew skills about halfway through the flight. I didn't have the confidence to talk very much, but from all the tapes I'd been listening to that summer, my comprehension of spoken Hebrew was strong enough to have a conversation.

A soon as I opened my mouth, the passengers around me began

peppering me with questions about my reasons for going to the Holy Land.

"I'm going into the army," I said, using one of the few Hebrew phrases I had down pat.

Jews being Jews—and let's be honest, gossip is one of our greatest, if least flattering, attributes—the word spread through the aisles in staccato Hebrew. All of a sudden, I had my own little fan club on the plane. Once the word got out, once everybody got wind that there was some little punk from L.A. making aliyah and committed to joining the IDF, I became the center of attention. Complete strangers were walking down the aisle, patting me on the shoulder, lighting my cigarette, telling me what a mitzvah, or good deed, I was doing.

One older man who'd served in the military with the Golani Brigade during the 1960s shook his head sadly and told me I was like a salmon swimming against the current, that the younger generation in Israel had lost all sense of communal values.

"These kids in Israel today," he said, shrugging. "No one wants to work on the kibbutzim anymore. No one wants to volunteer for the most dangerous Special Forces units. They do their service, sure, because it's mandatory, but they'd rather be a truck driver, a mess-hall cook, or a *jobnik*." That was the first time I'd encountered the pejorative Israeli slang that roughly means *flying a desk* during one's army service. The whole flight was just so *Israeli*. People were swapping seats with strangers, being rude and disruptive, but I loved the chaos. *Holy shit*, I kept thinking. *Everybody* here is Jewish. *Everyone* speaks Hebrew. I'm going to be a *citizen* and in a few more months, I'm going to be a *soldier*.

We landed at Ben-Gurion Airport at ten or eleven o'clock in the morning. The plane came to a halt and the doors opened. Blistering-hot wind rushed through the cabin like a fist, knocking out the trapped stale air we'd been breathing for twelve hours, and carrying the scent of ancient deserts and palm trees, of sweet figs growing on the shores of the Mediterranean Sea. The pilot's voice came over the speakers, giving his spiel in Hebrew, then again in English, then in French. He said it was nearly 40 degrees Celsius outside, about 105 degrees Fahrenheit.

They wheeled old-fashioned stairs up to the plane's door and, a few minutes later, I was standing on Israeli soil. The heat bounced off the tarmac and traveled up through my Nikes until the soles of my feet felt like they were going to melt. I saw the border patrol Jeeps circling around each flight, and realized that we were being scrutinized by soldiers carrying M-16s.

Then I saw a patrol of Blue Police—a group of eighteen- and nineteen-year-old border guards—and I couldn't believe that women so beautiful could actually be working as soldiers.

I made my way through the snaking immigration line where a young Sephardic woman was stamping people's passports. Before I even got to the front of the line, I'd heard her being a hard-ass, muttering her questions in a distinctly Moroccan-accented Hebrew—an accent I'd come to recognize well from my Ulpan classes in Los Angeles.

When I got to the front of the line, she was rude and abrupt—but I was laughing inside! I was so goddamn happy she was giving me her bullshit, pissy attitude. I was thinking, *Yes, this is what I'm talking about! This is Israel! This Sephardic chick right here in front of me—her fucking attitude, her aggressiveness—this is the real deal.*

"Why are you here?"

"Because I'm making aliyah."

"Yes, I know. I can read. But *why* have you made aliyah?"

"Because I want to go into the army."

Thick Moroccan lashes, framing eyes that shot me a cold, sarcastic look.

"So why didn't you just join the *American* army?"

"Because Israel's military is the best in the world," I said. "Because it takes a real *macher* to come enlist in the Israeli army."

She smiled finally, because I'd thrown some Yiddish at her along with the wise-ass attitude. I smiled back. I just wanted her to know that I knew the rules, that I *liked* the fact that she was breaking my balls. Because here was someone breaking my balls for a real reason. This was security with a *purpose*. This wasn't standing outside of a club in Beverly Hills or West Hollywood taking shit from a 270-pound douche bag of a doorman. She was doing her job in the most thorough way possible; grilling me, reading my eye movements, mentally running a psychological profile to determine if I'm legit or if I'm some kind of unhinged terrorist.

At last, she stamped my passport and welcomed me to the Holy Land.

As I took my first steps as an Israeli—I could hardly believe I was now officially a citizen—images from the books I'd read kept flooding into my mind. I remembered pictures of the Japanese Red Army terrorists who'd opened fire at the airport baggage claim in 1972. It was one of the biggest terrorist attacks of the 1970s: three Japanese gunmen, recruited by the Popular Front for the Liberation of Palestine, landed on an Air France flight from Paris, pulled out automatic guns and hand grenades, and started firing wildly, killing twenty-six people and injuring dozens more.*

This is where the massacre went down. I'm walking right on the scene of the slaughter.

There was no marker or memorial plaque. But to me, it was sacred ground.

* The attack took place on May 30, 1972, when the airport was known as Lod. At the time, Israeli airport security focused primarily on Palestinian threats, so the Japanese Red Army terrorists took them by surprise. Kozo Okamoto, Tsuyoshi Okudaira, and Yasuyuki Yasuda, trained in Lebanon, dressed as businessmen and carrying slim cases, attracted little attention before they opened fire. The victims included sixteen Christian pilgrims from Puerto Rico, and professor Aharon Katzir, an internationally renowned protein biophysicist.

FOUR

Outside the airport, a woman, tall, slim, dirty blond, in her late forties, stood holding up a piece of paper with my name written in black felt pen. I grabbed my duffel bag from the carousel and shouted her name. Sara Eisner was the wife of a famous Holocaust survivor named Jack Eisner. My stepfather had written the script for a movie of Eisner's life called *War and Love,* and when my stepfather contacted Sara before I left Los Angeles, she'd kindly offered to drive me up to the north of Israel and drop me off at the kibbutz.

Driving up the highway from Ben-Gurion Airport, I was so exhausted that I started to nod off, but then Sara began to point out various famous historical sites. The beach stretched out on our left and the dappled Mediterranean Sea was the deepest shade of blue. We passed the exit to Qalqilia, which lies on the westernmost edge of the territories. Only about two hundred feet separate Israeli land from Qalqilia in the West Bank. As I saw those signs in Arabic, I had the strange feeling that I was going to wind up there one day. And I did—many, many times.

As we traveled farther north, we passed an Arab town called Umm El-Fahem, which Sara explained was an Arab-Israeli settlement. The residents were Muslims but they held Israeli citizenship.

Shit, I thought, staring ahead. *I have so much to learn.* Sara told me about the various Arab communities within Israel's borders. Despite the animosity, sometimes open hatred between the groups, there's also a complex coexistence that can seem incomprehensible to outsiders. For example, the Christian Arabs, the Bedouins (who are also Arabs), and the Druze (who are often mistaken for Muslims, though they have their own distinct Semitic culture), all send their sons and daughters to serve alongside Jews in the Israeli army.

We passed Megiddo, the legendary battlefield, whose rocky soil has been fought over for millennia. The site is Har Megiddo, which is translated in the New Testament as Armageddon, the scene of the final battle between the forces of good and evil according to the Book of Revelation. But to modern-day Israelis, the fertile countryside around Megiddo is farm country, a kind of Kibbutz Lane.

The kibbutz I had signed up to work at was named Kibbutz Ha-Zorea. It was located on the slopes of the Carmel Mountains, about thirty-five kilometers south of Haifa, in stunning country west of the Sea of Galilee.

We arrived at the kibbutz gates and pulled up to a guardhouse. The guard came down to look in our window, toting an Uzi, but I remember laughing silently: The guy was wearing navy-blue Speedos and a sun-bleached blue tank top while shouldering his submachine gun.

Sara spoke to the guard in broken Hebrew. She had a strong Polish accent that didn't sound like the textbook Hebrew I'd been studying on my tapes, but it was enough to get us through the security checkpoint and into the kibbutz. After Sara dropped me off in front of the Admin Building, a woman named Eliza came out to take charge of me. She was in her early forties, with longish blond hair, and she walked around barefoot, looking like a typical farm *frau*. At first I thought she might be a *shiksa*, a convert to Judaism, but I was dead wrong. It turned out that Eliza had been an Israeli intelligence operative. An American who had made aliyah about twenty-five years earlier, on the same program that I was on, Eliza ended up marrying one of the kibbutzniks and making her life at Kibbutz Ha-Zorea. In Israel, I was to learn, you don't get far making snap judgments about people.

Eliza led me into a dormitory-style building, the residence for the Ulpan Hebrew-immersion kids and for all kibbutz volunteers, and left me at my bunk.

"Call me if you need anything," she said. "Tomorrow morning, we'll meet at my office at nine o'clock and I'll get you set up with your job."

Kibbutz Ha-Zorea was founded by Eastern European Zionists in the mid-1930s. Like all the kibbutzim, it was an experiment in socialist, collectivized living. No one owned any personal possessions. Everything was shared. Even cars were signed out and collectively owned by the kibbutz. They raised most of their own food, but their main moneymaker was raising exotic tropical fish for export.

When I left L.A., I assumed I would be working in those

fishponds, but when I reported to Eliza's office that first morning, she assigned me to the kitchen. I was pretty deflated but I didn't bitch and moan. I worked that detail for the next two or three weeks, scrubbing pots and scouring grills with the other American-born volunteers, a bunch of kids from Michigan State and NYU on various overseas programs. No one complained about the work—that would have been unacceptable on a kibbutz. Still, I hated being on the bottom rung like that when I felt I had so much more to offer.

After several weeks of learning the kibbutz hierarchy, I'd noticed that two of the main guys in the fishponds were brothers named Eyal and Arnon Weiss. I'd been told all the Weiss brothers had been officers in the Special Forces. Their father had been an officer, too, apparently a legend in the old days.

It drove me insane that there was a whole generation of warriors working right on the kibbutz with me while I was stuck on kitchen duty all day long, scrubbing baked ziti off industrial pans.

I wanted so badly to work in the fishponds, but one thing kept holding me back. I remembered what the little general said, sitting poolside at my parents' place in Beverly Hills:

"And, Aaron, when you get there—listen to me now—don't be a big shot, okay?"

Eyal Weiss ran the fishponds with another ex-commando named Gali. They did such grueling physical work—swimming for upwards of twelve hours a day and dragging hundreds of pounds of fish in the nets through the freezing water—that even in their forties, their bodies looked like they'd been chiseled from granite. They were aloof and unapproachable, like shirtless rock stars.

My frustration was mounting daily. The only thing I was getting out of the kitchen detail was dishpan hands, but I was scared of the consequences of trying to talk to the ex-commandos. The Weiss brothers had reputations as serious bad-asses. Would they brush me aside with a sneer? Could they have me demoted to something worse—like cleaning the bathrooms or being on garbage detail? Or maybe one of them would decide to put me in my place.

Finally one morning, after scrubbing the breakfast dishes for hours, something came over me. I walked straight up to Eyal Weiss and introduced myself as Aaron Cohen from California.

"Listen, man," I said, speaking in my pathetic broken Hebrew. "I'm going into the army in November. I don't know how to say this, but I didn't come here to clean pots and pans, you know? I'd like to work with you guys in the fishponds."

At the time, I didn't realize what a ballsy—what an *insane*—move this was. I mean, people don't just walk up to an ex-Special Forces officer like Eyal and start shooting the shit. Most volunteers on the kibbutz never opened their mouths. The attitude was, "You're getting a free meal. Shut your goddamn mouth and do your assigned job."

Eyal didn't smile or give me so much as a nod in reply. I had no idea what was going through his mind. Maybe he thought I was a typical American asshole. Maybe he thought I was a nut job. Then he just turned and walked away.

There was a heavyset Moroccan girl in charge of all the work assignments. She couldn't stand me and the feeling was mutual. I thought she was a loudmouth and a power-hungry control freak. For weeks, I'd been pleading with her to give me some manual labor—even farmwork—instead of the mindless kitchen detail but she wouldn't even think of changing my work assignment. Now, by talking to Eyal Weiss directly, I'd gone over her head. I could tell word had gotten back to her from glances she shot me in the cafeteria later that day. She was furious.

The next morning, she walked over to me. "Cohen, come with me," she said. "You're in the fishponds from now on."

I was so happy I could have hugged her, but she kept glaring at me indignantly. Still, that was Lesson Number One in Israel: If you don't *ask*, you don't get. Actually, that's not quite right: If you don't ask the *right* person, you don't get.

It was a key moment in my Israeli journey, and a strategy I found I would have to employ over and over again in the months ahead. Without summoning the courage to forgo protocol, I never would have got a tryout for the Special Forces, let alone made it into the select ranks of a unit like Duvdevan.

FIVE

Besides the new fishpond work, I was going to my Ulpan classes, trying to become fluent in Hebrew before the army call-up several months away. I worked half the week at the fishpond, and went to school the other half. They put me in Kinder Alef, which is like first grade. I also started running eight miles and doing hundreds of push-ups and sit-ups a day in addition to swimming long hours in the fishponds. If I had a hope of passing muster at a Tier One tryout, my body would have to be "C-Kosher," as they say in Hebrew: utterly flawless, without a single chink in the armor.

My athletic regimen was the easy part: Any gym rat can transform his physique with a few months of intense training. Mastering modern Hebrew was a hell of a lot tougher. No matter how my grammar and syntax were improving, I couldn't *think* in the language, which left me floundering in linguistic quicksand every time

I had to open my mouth. And Israelis can be the most sarcastic, ill-mannered people on earth; if you get a phrase wrong in conversation, they won't bother to correct you or give you some brotherly advice. They'll laugh in your face, call you a stupid douche bag, shrug, and walk off.

But my *real* homework was researching the subtleties and interagency rivalries between the Special Forces units. I read and reread all the history books and culled as much information as I could from the ex-commandos themselves in an effort to figure out which unit was right for me.

As I've said, the big three of the Israeli Special Forces community are the Sayeret Matkal, Sayeret Shaldag, and Shayetet-13. Matkal's main functions today are counterterrorism, hostage rescue, deep reconnaissance, and intelligence gathering. Among the prominent Matkalists are former prime ministers Ehud Barak, Ariel Sharon, and Benjamin "Bibi" Netanyahu. Bibi's older brother, Yonatan Netanyahu, was the heroic unit commander killed at Entebbe.

Sayeret Shaldag (or Unit 5101) is the Israel Air Force's Special Operations Unit. Founded in 1974, the unit engages in missions throughout the Middle East involving ground-based designation for air-to-ground laser-guided munitions, often infiltrating enemy territory to precisely mark targets for the Air Force's F-16s to strike later. Recently, Shaldag has expanded its responsibilities to include counterterrorism and hostage rescue operations.

Shayetet-13 (generally abbreviated as "S-13") was formed in 1949 and has earned a worldwide reputation for their daring naval raids and underwater commando operations. Aside from being the

Navy's elite unit for special missions, S-13 is also a top-level counterterrorism unit, often executing covert ops deep within enemy territory and combining assault by sea, land, and air. Of all the guys I worked with at the fishpond, the S-13 veterans maintained the most impressive physical regimen. The Weiss brothers were like dolphins in the water, graceful, acrobatic, preternaturally strong and completely comfortable freezing their balls off at four in the morning. Physically speaking, S-13 offered inarguably the hardest training block in the IDF.

I began riding down to the fishponds every morning with the commandos. The workers were primarily veterans of Sayeret Matkal and Shayetet-13. These were the guys I'd been dreaming of coming to Israel to learn from ever since reading books about their exploits back at Robert Land Academy. Working in the fishponds attracted the former commandos on the kibbutzim because they were the type of men who didn't shy away from physical labor and, as I was soon to learn, an extraordinary level of physical fitness was required to do the work.

We were farming koi, a species of exotic carp, and a very popular aquarium fish which the kibbutz shipped all over the world. The fish were raised in massive football-field-sized ponds. There were roughly forty of these fishponds. The koi were the kibbutz's most lucrative cash crop, so only the best workers made the cut because the kibbutz didn't want even a single fish to get killed by accident.

Among the thirty guys who worked at the fishponds were the Weiss brothers, Eyal and Arnon, who were ex–Shayetet-13 commandos; David and Gali, who were technically the bosses (though this being a socialist commune, there wasn't a formal chain of command), and an ex-commando named Dror Shapiro, whom I held in awe because he'd been part of the Matkal team who'd gone into Entebbe in 1976. Dror was in his mid-forties when I met him, rail-thin, fit as an Olympic decathlete, always wearing a pair of cheesy aviator sunglasses with the leather horse-blinder attachments on the sides. Despite his gruff exterior, I became very close to Dror during those months on the kibbutz.

The routine was this: Up at four A.M. Travel about a kilometer down a winding dirt path to the refinery, where the fish were sorted. It was still pitch-dark when we got to work, and we jumped into that freezing water wearing only a pair of Speedos, rubber boots, and industrial rubber gloves. For the rest of the workday, we were either sorting or fishing. We were split into teams and throughout the day, each team was required to make four or five pulls. We would take a huge net and wade into the pond, sweeping the net toward the opposite side, cornering and corralling the fish into one corner. Each pull required us to swim sixty or seventy yards in murky, ice-cold water.

One of the first things I had to learn was to cover my balls with one hand so the carp's dorsal fin didn't puncture one of my testicles. Once we began rounding up the fish into one corner of the pond, we continually staked the net into place, making it smaller and smaller. Then we had to jump inside the net and scoop the fish into buckets. Koi aren't little goldfish or guppies. They are about a foot and half long, with a razor-sharp dorsal fin, and a tendency to thrash violently when caught. The first time I waded into the midst of those churning fish, I reeled back, having been nipped in the thigh. It was a deep cut. Warm blood billowed into the water in clouds.

"Fuck!" I shouted.

One of the ex-Matkal guys was laughing hysterically. "Aaron, man! *Al tishkach lishmor al ha beytzim shelcha!* Make sure you cover your nuts, huh?"

It usually took us a good hour and a half to get the net cinched and begin culling the best fish. That's when the real backbreaking labor began. Forming a human chain of six or seven guys, we started passing buckets, hand-to-hand, filled with the wildly thrashing fish all the way back up to the refinery, an exhausting process that lasted for hours.

It was high-intensity work: swimming, sweating, chasing fish all day. Working steadily from dawn until three-thirty or four P.M., I found I could pack away four or five pounds of food a day—my metabolism was on overdrive. By the time I returned to my bunk around six P.M., I was dead to the world. I literally wouldn't move from my bed until the alarm sounded in the morning.

The commandos were incessantly busting my balls about my bad Hebrew, teasing me, communicating only in their own bad English. "Speak to me in Hebrew," I kept saying, but they continued to talk only in broken English. Theirs was a closed, tight-knit fraternity, and they wanted me to know I was an outsider, not worthy to be spoken to in their native language.

At least I'd lasted through the initiation phase. The handful of American kids who were given a shot to work in the fishponds had all been drummed out after a short spell. Outsider or not, I took great pride in being the only American to tough it out.

One morning we were told to shoot a flock of pelicans that had been eating too many of our prized koi. An ex-commando named

Uri, who'd served in a tank unit doing Special Forces reconnaissance, handed me a 12-gauge shotgun.

"Aaron, come with me," Uri said. "Can you shoot?"

"Yeah, I can handle it."

I stood aiming the gun when I realized Uri was staring at me.

"Aaron, why you came here to join the army? You fucking *crazy* or something?"

I just smiled, loading up the gun with buckshot and handing it back to him.

"Why would you want to come here when every Israeli is trying to get to New York or L.A.? I mean, here everyone's born into the army life, why would you want to come to this?"

Everybody thought I was either certifiably insane or some kind of idiot. That was the general attitude until the day I finished my training. There was no real explanation I could give them, at least not one they'd accept. Everybody just thought: That Cohen kid, he's got a screw loose.

As he got to know me better, Uri started to school me, doling out tidbits of advice. After a couple of weeks of working together, he took me aside during one of our walks.

"Listen, Aaron," he said. "When you're at the *gibush**—I can see what you're made of now, and I'm confident you're going to get a shot at a *gibush*—the instructors are going to play games with you. And, no matter what, don't quit. That's all they want to see. They're just testing you."

I was staring at him, not asking any questions, taking it all in.

---

* *Gibush* refers to a highly selective, brutal tryout for the Israeli Special Forces and other elite all-volunteer military units.

"No matter what they say, even if they give you the option of walking away, don't quit. They'll scream at you, 'Asshole, if you don't leave, we're taking you to jail!' And, Aaron, you remember this well: Tell them, 'I'm here. I'm staying.'"

One thing a casual reader must understand about Israel in the mid-1990s, a fact which is even more true today: The spirit of the pioneering kibbutzniks was dying off, if not completely dead. According to one of the leading academic experts on sociology, politics, and crime in Israel, Professor Shlomo Giora Shoham of Tel Aviv University, the crisis in Israel today is one of declining values among the younger generation. Shoham, the former assistant attorney general of Israel, is the author of over seventy books and chairman of the university's criminology department. His son, a Special Forces soldier, was killed in Egypt during the Yom Kippur War in 1973.

"We've become a country of extremes, rich and poor," Shoham said recently.* "And if you're poor in this country, well, you're better off dead." A dour, bearded seventy-two-year-old, he railed against the breakdown of cultural values in Israel, particularly among the youth, like some Old Testament prophet. "There's nothing to stop them, there are no boundaries, there are no limits. And as Ivan Karamazov said, 'If everything is possible, then nothing is true.'"

The socialist-Zionist communes were once synonymous with the pioneering spirit of the newly founded State of Israel, but the idea of shared sacrifice is no longer glamorous to young Israelis, and kibbutzim

---

* Interview at Shoham's home in north Tel Aviv with Aaron Cohen's coauthor, Douglas Century.

increasingly are forced to hire Palestinian Arabs and immigrants from Africa and Asia to do the manual labor and farmwork. "The young are going for the quick kicks, gambling, and sex and hedonism. The highest rate of drug addiction is in the kibbutzim these days," Professor Shoham said. "There was a time when the army was a great value. Our greatest value. But right now there are almost no volunteers to the crack units. The Orthodox are practically the only ones volunteering."

A few months into my kibbutz stint on the fishpond, my container crate finally arrived. Inside was my candy-apple red Suzuki motorcycle. I wasn't trying to be some kind of show-off. Israel is a small country, but the public transportation isn't all that reliable. You can't get around the country that easily without having transportation, especially coming home from the Army on weekend leave when all you want to do is sleep and wash your dirty military fatigues.

The kibbutz administrators liked me and saw how hard I worked, but when my motorcycle showed up, everyone freaked out. Five administrators circled me, yelling all at once: "You can't have that here, Cohen! This is a kibbutz!"

"We share cars here, you idiot! You have to sign them out—you know that, right?"

"Well," I said. "I don't get to sign out a car, I'm not a kibbutznik."

"That's right. You're not a kibbutznik. You're just a volunteer. And now you're going into the army. You're a lonely soldier on the kibbutz, and these are the privileges you get. You can't keep a motorcycle here. Case closed."

SIX

My stepfather's friends Jack and Sara Eisner lived in the Mediterranean coastal town of Caesarea. After I settled in to life on the kibbutz, Jack and Sara extended an open invitation to weekly Shabbat dinners. It was at one of these Friday-night meals in Caesaria that I met a soft-spoken woman who would change my life.

Golda, who had also survived the Holocaust as a child, hidden by a Christian family, was in her early seventies, small, delicate, and white-haired. She still spoke Hebrew with a pronounced Polish-Yiddish accent. Over the course of my first year in Israel, she became my mentor, my confidante, my second Jewish mother. To look at Golda you might think she was the typical Yiddish-speaking *bubbeh*, dispensing advice with a half-smile, resting her 118 pounds on a blue metal cane, limping noticeably but stoically on a prosthetic left hip.

But she was no ordinary Jewish grandmother. Golda was an intelligence operative, one of Israel's longest-serving and most highly decorated Mossad agents. Twenty years earlier, she'd been crippled, left for dead, her hip smashed to pieces by Arab terrorists while she was on a deep-cover mission in North Africa. She'd been friends with leading Israeli politicians and generals and was especially close to Prime Minister Yitzhak Rabin in the years before his assassination. Now semiretired, she still kept a desk at Mossad headquarters in Tel Aviv.

Every few weeks, for Shabbat, I used to ask for a leave from the kibbutz. I'd jump on my bike and ride ninety minutes to her apartment in northern Tel Aviv. I met Golda's son and his girlfriend. We smoked a lot of cigarettes, drank a lot of coffee, and Golda made me feel like a member of the family.

Just like the little general I'd met back in Beverly Hills, Golda was noncommittal. She couldn't make any promises. If she could help me, she said with a shrug, she would make a few calls, do her best to arrange an invitation for me to attend the Wingate Institute for a *gibush*. I thanked her profusely, but told her that I wanted to try to do this one solo. I wanted to succeed or fail on my own abilities and merits, without calling in the help of my parents or any of their friends.

Not long after first landing in Israel, I'd reported to the *Lishkat Hagius*, or local army induction center, to open a file and start the process for my army call-up. Six months later, I finally got a notice in the mail to report for my testing.

For the first phase of testing, I traveled to Rechov Elhadif in the city of Tiberias, on the Sea of Galilee. In addition to the medical exam, the Israel Defense Forces do the most extensive academic and psychological evaluations in the world, starting with an all-purpose evaluation, called the "Psychometric"—a rough equivalent of the American SATs—which test vocabulary, grammar, and reading comprehension.

Several weeks later, I received another notice to report for advanced testing. The letter didn't specify what this second phase was for, but when I showed it to Arnon Weiss, he nodded.

"That's the psychological test—for Matkal and the pilots."

I was so pumped, I could have hugged Arnon. But he just offered another nod; he knew that I still had a long haul before even being granted the right to try out for a Special Forces unit.

Even more than the Special Forces fighters, the Israeli Air Force pilots have extraordinarily precise standards, and they've devised intelligence and aptitude tests with bizarre shapes, blocks, and puzzles to measure visual perception, organization, and countless forms of nonverbal problem solving. Despite the nonverbal component, my Hebrew was still so poor I could never have completed the four-hour test in Hebrew. But they'd actually arranged a special version for me with English-language instructions and answers.

A few more weeks passed, and yet another tan envelope arrived on my bunk at the kibbutz. I was now being ordered to report for my first day at the basic recruiting depot, known in Hebrew as the *Basis Klitah Umiun* but almost always referred to as the Bakum.

This was it—whatever unit I landed in, I would from that day forward be an Israel Defense Forces soldier. I said my good-byes around the kibbutz, gave the commandos a few hugs, then got on the bus. Dror Shapiro told me again and again that he was confident I'd get a shot at the *gibush* for Matkal or another of the Special Forces units.

I was psyched, but I had no clue what was going to happen to me from this point forward. When you get to the Bakum, first off, they ask you to list your top three choices of where you want to serve. I'd met and come to respect great fighters from Matkal, Shaldag, Shayetet-13, from the paratroopers, Golani Brigade, and regular tank battalions as well. But there was no doubt in my mind, at that stage, that the gold standard among the Special Forces hierarchy was Sayeret Matkal.

On the kibbutz, the Matkalists, by and large, had kept themselves apart. Among the commando society, they were sometimes derided as pretty boys and intellectuals, but there was still no denying that Matkalists were regarded as the most respected and secretive unit, a reputation that created a serious rift with S-13.

Each unit has an unofficial motto. Matkal's is: *Whatever doesn't go with strength, goes with brains.* And the motto of S-13, deliberately mocking Matkal, is: *Whatever doesn't go with strength, goes with more strength.*

There was a popular joke that said Matkal had been ordered to move a wall from Tel Aviv to Jerusalem. Matkal took the wall apart, hit it with sledgehammers, and rebuilt it perfectly in Jerusalem. S-13, on the other hand, given the same orders, opted for the more direct approach: they pushed the whole fucking wall from Tel Aviv to Jerusalem.

Of course, both units have had incredible success on dangerous operations. And both units have powerful political lobbies working to get them those missions.

When I had to list my top three preferences for placement, I had no doubts. Neither did I have a fall-back plan.

"Sayeret Matkal, Sayeret Matkal, and Sayeret Matkal," I wrote as I awaited my introductory interview with a second lieutenant. "Those are my three choices. Those are my *only* choices."

I wasn't trying to be a smart-ass; that's the way I was told to play it. All the ex-Matkalists on the kibbutz coached me to stick to my guns. "Don't back down," Dror and Uri often said. "Eventually you'll get to where you want to go."

Next, I was thrown in a big tent, issued all the basic gear, and then I just hung around for a few days, bouncing between medical checks and psychological tests. Every eighteen-year-old Israeli kid comes through that base. It's a real meat-grinder of conscripts: kids who are super-gung-ho to serve; kids who'd give anything in the world to get out of serving; mostly kids who just don't give a shit one way or the other.

I got to my interview and suddenly I was sitting in front of the second lieutenant who was reviewing my file, analyzing my aptitude and psychological test scores, smiling when he saw that I'd written Sayeret Matkal as my first, second, and third choices.

"So what's the deal, Cohen?" the second lieutenant asked.

My Hebrew was still pretty broken but I managed to explain myself. "I came from the United States. to volunteer for the Army. I made aliyah. I want a *gibush*. I want a shot at trying out for the unit."

You never say the names of the Special Forces units in conversation, by the way. Especially not with a senior officer. Matkal is often just referred to by its numerical designation, "Two-Six."

The second lieutenant hadn't seen too many cases like mine before. "So you could have gone to college in the States, but you chose to come here? Well, good for you," he said. Then he let out a sigh. "The problem is I can't do it. I can't offer you the *gibush* you're requesting. But I can give you any other unit you want. I'll send you to Golani or I'll send you to Givati," he continued, referring to two of the IDF's infantry regiments. "Any fighting unit you want, it's yours."

"I didn't come here to serve in the regular infantry, sir. I came here to try out for the Special Forces. I'd like the same opportunity that every Israeli gets. I want a tryout. That's all I'm asking."

"Let me see what I can do," he grumbled.

For the next few days, I hung around, sleeping in a tent, doing nothing, desperate for a decision. Hundreds of other recruits were sitting around like me, waiting to get taken off in buses to basic training. After a week, I was starting to get worried. Finally, the second lieutenant called me back to his office where I found myself standing in front of the second lieutenant and his superior officer, a captain. Both men were staring hard at me, looking like the bearers of bad news.

"We've got no tryouts for you, Cohen," the captain said. "But here's what we're going to do: A lot of the American kids get sent to Nahal, which is a fighting unit that was developed to protect the kibbutzim in the north. Nahal's got a lot of history, a lot of pride." I knew that Nahal soldiers got to wear the coveted red boots, designating elite-unit status, but still, I wasn't having it.

"No disrespect, sir, but I didn't come here to serve alongside other Americans," I said. "I came here to have a shot at an elite unit. I want a tryout. Let that tryout decide where you send me."

I was being polite, but this was borderline insubordination. Yet I was resolute: I'd traveled seventy-five hundred miles, left my family and friends behind, forgone a college education, worked my ass off in the freezing waters of a kibbutz fishpond, and immersed myself for months in a foreign language—I didn't do all this just to serve in one of the basic infantry units, driving a truck or serving as a mess-hall cook.

"I want a tryout for the unit," I said again. "That's what I came here to do."

The captain was also sticking to his guns. "This is the best we can offer you, Cohen. Dismissed."

I went back to the tent, feeling disconsolate. But I felt a hell of a lot worse when my name got called again a few hours later. The officers had closed the file on me; they were sending me to do my basic training with Nahal Brigade.

"Cohen, get on board the bus!" a sergeant was shouting.

"No."

"What did you say, Cohen? Get on the bus!"

"No, I'm not going to Nahal," I said.

"Really, big shot? You're not getting on the bus? Then you're going to the brig."

The sergeant was about to call in the military police. I had one option left. I almost passed out with relief when Golda picked up her phone in Tel Aviv.

"Hey, it's Aaron," I said, trying to keep my desperation to a whisper. I was supposed to be boarding the Nahal-bound bus at that very instant, and I wasn't sure who was looking over my shoulder, or listening.

"What's wrong, Aaron?"

"I'm at the Bakum right now. They're about to ship me off to Nahal," saying it out loud made the precariousness of my position terrifyingly real to me. I had to make sure that Golda understood what this meant to me. "Listen," I continued, my voice rising. "I'm not getting on that fucking bus. They'll send me to the brig, I'll do my stint in military jail, and head back to L.A. I didn't come all this way to get sent to the regular infantry. I've been prepping a year for this!"

"Okay, Aaron, okay," Golda said calmly, trying to reassure me that things would work out. "Stay where you are. And no matter what, don't get on the bus. Even if they try to drag you, don't get on. If you get on the bus, I can't help you anymore. It will be too late by then. Now let me see what I can do."

So I sat on the dirt outside the bus with my duffel bag and kept refusing orders to get onboard. The officers were glaring at me; I thought I was going to get muscled off to the brig at any minute.

Instead, not more than twenty minutes later, this skinny NCO came running up to me, waving his arms frantically. Golda had worked her Mossad magic.

"Aaron Cohen! Aaron Cohen!" the NCO was shouting. "Which one is Aaron Cohen?"

"I'm right here."

All of a sudden, I felt like I could breathe again. I stood up from my crouch, brushed the sand and dirt from my fatigues.

"You need to come with me right now!"

He brought me straight to the commanding officer of the whole Bakum. "When you come before the general, soldier," the NCO whispered, "salute."

I wasn't even formally in the army yet and I hadn't been taught how to salute. "Okay, fine," I whispered back.

Boom, next thing I knew, I was standing in front of this suntanned general, short and portly, with a severe, raised-eyebrow expression.

"What's going on here?" he muttered in Hebrew. He glanced at my file, shifted mid-thought to perfect, slightly accented English. "You came here from the States?"

"Yes, sir."

"Okay, you've got a date for a *gibush.*"

He held up a piece of paper, reached over his desk and handed it to me, mumbling something I couldn't understand in Hebrew. It took me a minute to translate the orders—*Aaron Cohen is hereby ordered to report to the main entrance, Wingate Institute, Netanya, 42902 for an official Elite Units Testing and Selection Tryout*—but then it was all I could do not to break into an ear-to-ear grin.

SEVEN

Located on the Mediterranean coast, just south of the city of Netanya, the Wingate Institute is the country's most prestigious sports academy, the training site for Israel's leading athletes as well as top European soccer clubs. Once a year, Wingate hosts tryouts (or *gibushim*) for Israel's military pilots and Special Forces commandos. Less than 5 percent of those invited to the Wingate Institute complete the weeklong ordeal.

Though not Jewish, Orde Charles Wingate (1903–1944) was—and remains—a towering legend of the Israeli military establishment. Born in India, Wingate was a devout Protestant who received a strict religious education, and who rose to the rank of major-general in the British army during World War II. In 1936, he became an intelligence officer and was assigned to Palestine. From his arrival in the Holy Land, he saw the creation of a Jewish state in Palestine as a literal fulfillment of Christian prophecy and immediately allied himself with the leaders of the Haganah. At the time, Arab guerrillas had begun a campaign of attacks, known as the Arab Revolt, against both British mandate officials and the Jewish communities. Wingate formulated an idea of armed groups of British-trained Jewish commandos, known as the Special Night Squads—in a sense, the forerunners to Israel's modern-day Special Forces units. It was the first instance of the British recognizing the Haganah's legitimacy as a Jewish defense force. Wingate trained, commanded, and accompanied the Special Night Squads on their patrols, ambushing Arab saboteurs and raiding border villages. However, his deepening political involvement with the Zionist cause, and an incident where he spoke publicly in favor of formation of a Jewish state while on leave in Britain, forced his superiors in Palestine to remove him from command. Even in his absence, Wingate remained beloved by many of the early Zionist fighters. Moshe Dayan, who had trained under him, later claimed that militarily speaking, Wingate "taught us everything we know."

When I showed up for the *gibush* at the institute, I wasn't thinking too much about Wingate's influence in the history of Zionism or the IDF. I was simply nervous. Or more accurately, I was scared shitless. Uri's words echoed in my head constantly:

When you're at the gibush . . . no matter what . . . don't quit. Tell them, "I'm here. I'm staying."

Our *gibush* started with over two hundred guys—all pumped,

frenzied, confident, sweating testosterone. We wore vests and fatigues, and had a numbered sticker on our helmets. We camped outside in tents and slept right on the sand.

Barely slept, I should say. If I was lucky, I might drift off for four hours of exhausted unconsciousness. The officers pushed us through twenty-hour days of nonstop running, push-ups, and situps. Then they threw in one sleepless twenty-four-hour hell day. It was a living nightmare: screaming, stress, agony, depression, tears.

Every aspect of your character, as well as your physical and mental fortitude, is being tested: Integrity. Stamina. Honesty. Teamwork. Thinking under pressure. Situational awareness. The instructors are breaking you down, trying to trip you up, getting to your inner core: *Who are you?* And I had the added stressor of being screamed at 24/7 in Hebrew.

On the fourth day, during one of our marathon runs, I fell hard on some rocks and immediately knew my ankle was fucked. By that evening, my foot was turning purple and had ballooned to twice its normal size. I packed the sprain with ice, wrapped it in tensor bandages. *Fuck it,* I figured. *If I have to hop, I'll hop.* There was no way I was going to quit.

The medic in my tent had other ideas. "You're done, Cohen," he said. "I can't sign off on you in this condition."

There were only three days left, and from the two hundred revved-up guys at the start, we were down to twenty-four survivors. After the medic left, I lay quietly on my bunk for a few minutes. Then I looked at the pile of empty helmets from the dozens of guys who'd been injured, sent home, or broken down emotionally.

"Listen up, fuckhead," I barked at myself. "You aren't going home.

You've come too far. You're not going back to L.A. You are *not* going to *quit*."

I put my vest and helmet back on, took the sticker off the helmet of one of the drop-outs, and stuck it on mine. I figured the trick might buy me a few hours, get me through the rest of the day. I sneaked back in formation. I managed to pull it off for about twenty minutes, until we were ordered to undertake a brutal uphill run carrying buckets of sand. Seeing me hopping on one leg, the instructor started shouting:

"What the fuck is going on here?"

His name was Udi. A veteran of Sayeret Matkal, Udi was in his late thirties, deeply tanned, short but thickly muscled like a middleweight boxer. On the bridge of his nose, thick black eyebrows came to an unruly union.

"What are *you* doing here?" Udi was so enraged the spittle was flying in my face.

"I thought we told you to go home. Go back to the tent. You're done!"

"All due respect, sir, just because you say I'm done doesn't mean I'm done. It's my body. I know my body and I know when I'm done."

"Aaron, stop being a big shot," he said quietly. "Stop being a tough guy. You did a good job, you lasted four days, you showed you got *ometz*"—Hebrew slang for guts—"I'll recommend you for something else. Don't worry, you'll get a good placement. Now get out. You're gonna injure yourself worse."

"I'm not going anywhere, sir."

"If you don't go back to the tent right now, I'm gonna call the military police. They're gonna take you to jail and we'll let the court sort it out. Don't fuck with me."

"So tell them to come pick me up." At this point I was so sleep-deprived, exhausted, and delirious, I really *didn't* give a fuck what happened.

"You're not gonna go?" Without warning Udi sprang toward me, coiled in a boxer's crouch, then landed a vicious right-uppercut to my midsection. I fell on my ass, twisted to one side, crumpled, groaning, eyes streaming freely. "You're insubordinate," he said. "After you get out of the brig, they're gonna send your stupid ass back to California."

He left me there on the ground while the other twenty-three guys continued to train. Somehow I pulled myself together and started limping after them.

I hopped around for a day and a half. The military police never showed up. Dror and Uri were right. It was a mind game. Udi was putting me through a psychological test, seeing what kind of *ometz* I had, what it would take to break me. I sucked up the pain, finished the training block—always in last place, hopping on one foot. At night, I'd pop some aspirin with codeine from the medic's tent, and ice down my ankle before wrapping it in bandages.

On the final day at Wingate we had to complete a ten-kilometer march with heavy field gear. It took the other twenty-three guys two or three hours; it took me more than seven. Everyone was laughing, standing around a big buffet table, stuffing themselves with hummus, falafel, fresh fruit, and cake. Some of the guys were cheering me on; others were pointing, half-mocking smiles on their faces. I didn't really give a fuck. I grabbed a canteen of cold water, almost too exhausted to stand any longer.

Then Udi ordered us into formation.

"Listen, you all did a fantastic job making it through the week. Those of you who aren't selected, don't take it personally. Those who make the cut—congratulations."

Completing the physical week of the course is only one component of the selection process; to make it into a Tier One unit, a candidate must pass an extensive background check during which the commanding officers dig up everything they can about his past associations, family history, and school friends.

We were called one by one into Udi's office to hear the news. When they summoned me, I was in bad shape. I'd spent the last half hour throwing up and I was fairly certain I'd done some lasting damage by aggravating my sprained ankle. Udi was sitting at his desk. Another commando, a thin, blond-haired officer with pale blue eyes, stood behind him.

"We really like you, Aaron," Udi said. "We think you have a lot of balls, a lot of potential. But you're not for us. You're not for Matkal and you're not for Shaldag."

I stared at him, so disappointed and exhausted I was unable to speak.

"It's not your commitment; it's not your heart," Udi said. "You've got those in spades. But it comes down to this: You weren't born here. You aren't Israeli. Your family isn't Israeli. It'll be next to impossible to trace your background and family history with the requisite level of security. But we wanted to evaluate you in the training to see where you might fit. That's why I want to introduce you to a friend of mine, Ilan Rubenstein. He's from a very specialized unit that"—now Udi let out a small, sarcastic laugh, clearly about some private joke between them—"works very *closely* with the Arab community."

Udi wished me luck, shook my hand, and left. I was so crushed

I felt like crying. I'd just gone through the most physically grueling experience in my life and I wanted to shout: *Now* you tell me, you fuckin' hard-ass? *Now* you say that because I wasn't born here, because my family's not Israeli, you were *never* going to take me? *Cocksucker!* I knew that my getting into Matkal was a long shot—but you couldn't tell me this on day one or day two?

I didn't realize until later—once we'd become the tightest of friends—that Ilan's story was just like mine. He was born in Australia and had immigrated to Israel determined to get into an elite counterterrorism unit.

"Udi tells me that you showed some good qualities," Ilan said. "I'd like to give you the opportunity to train with us."

"Who are you guys?"

"I can't tell you that. I can only tell you who we are after you've been in the unit for eight months." He fixed his gaze on me, challenging me to look away. "You'll have to go through basic training all over again. You'll go back to the bottom. You'll sign up with the paratroopers and from the paratroopers we'll put you in a special platoon. If you make it through eight months there, only *then* will you find out who and what we are."

Ilan wasn't being overly secretive without reason. In Israel, no one is allowed to talk about any of the Special Forces units, even while you are in the process of training for them. In actuality, no one is told at the end of the Tier One tryout at Wingate where he or she will be assigned. You might have an idea—based on what kind of training you receive and what your top choices were back at the Bakum—but for the first eight months of basic training, you are *technically* not part of a specific unit.

I liked Ilan's plain-spoken manner as he gave me the lowdown.

In the months and years ahead, Ilan and I would become as close as brothers despite the fact that he was already an officer and I was just a lowly trainee. He'd also had his heart set on being a warrior with Matkal and found out the hard way, as I just had, that each of the Israeli Special Forces units has its own peculiar history and traditions. Sayeret Matkal is like a forty-year-old boys' club; to get into Matkal, you not only need to be born in Israel, you almost always have to be the son, nephew, or cousin of a former Matkalist.

Unlike me, Ilan had an Israeli-born father, an Ashkenazi who had grown up in Israel and served in the Israeli army. And Ilan had been extremely competitive with his father while growing up. His family was mainstream, prominent in the Melbourne Jewish community, but Ilan was something of a black sheep. Ilan's dad had been in a very tough unit, the Sayeret Tzanhanim, the paratrooper reconnaissance unit, in the 1960s and 1970s. Ilan grew up with stories of his father's exploits and he wanted to show his dad that he had the right stuff, too. He ended up doing far more than his dad ever did, becoming not just a Special Forces soldier, but a team leader and an officer, as well as the head of training at the Counter Terror School near the end of his career.

What created the intense bond between Ilan and me was that we were both foreigners. His spoken Hebrew was pitch-perfect, but his written Hebrew was as semi-illiterate as mine. Over the years we spent serving together, we never talked about our shared experience of being outsiders but it was a constant issue for both of us, one we counteracted with a kind of machismo, and a determination to get to that place where we were no longer looking at the fish swimming in the fishbowl. We both badly wanted to be *inside* the fishbowl.

Among all the *olim hadashim*, the new immigrants—whether it was on the kibbutz or in the regular IDF or in the elite Tier One units—there was a constant race to see who could learn Hebrew the best, who could integrate the quickest, who had the most natural Israeli mannerisms. Between Ilan and me, it became a good-natured contest, almost like a sibling rivalry, about who could better pass himself off as a natural-born Sabra.

But back at Wingate, Ilan's personality and family history were a mystery to me. The only hint I got was the faint trace of an Australian accent.

He was leaning back on Udi's desk, waiting for my response about returning to basic training to await his call to join this as-yet-unnamed unit. *Only then will you find out who and what we are . . .*

"Yalla," I said, an Arabic word which is common slang in Israel meaning "okay" or "sure." The truth was I was beyond exhausted, and so relieved that I wasn't going to be assigned a job as a truck-driver or an army cook, that I would have leapt at any opportunity, let alone one to serve in the Special Forces alongside an officer like Ilan.

PART II

EIGHT

"This is it," I told the old, white-bearded cabdriver with the blue-and-silver *chamsah*, or Hand of God, pendant dangling from his rearview mirror. "You can let me out here."

I'd given him only the vague directions that Ilan had given me: Take the highway between Tel Aviv and Jerusalem, slow down north of the Israeli town of Modi'in, and pull over next to the Palestinian village of Budrus.

But the cabbie knew exactly where he was taking me; like most Israelis, he understood full well what kind of training takes place at Beit Mitkan Adam. He was respectful enough not to ask me any questions about it during the forty-minute drive.

It was a bright winter morning when I first showed up at Mitkan Adam. The base, named for General Yekutiel "Kuti" Adam, the highest-ranking officer killed in action from 1982 to this day, is a sprawling Special Forces training facility, where between five and ten units cycle through over a five-month period. (Each unit is typically composed of two platoons, or *machlakot* in Hebrew, of between fifteen and twenty guys. Two platoons make up a *pluga*, or company.)

At the front gate, two fresh-faced eighteen-year-old guards checked my ID and sent me through. I walked a half-mile uphill, passing the Counter-Terror School on the left side, and the Sniper School on the right. But the thing that truly caught my attention—the most eye-grabbing detail, to be perfectly honest—were the women. Hot women. All over the base. It blew my mind! Everywhere you turned there were gorgeous, young, tanned female conscripts working as support staff and instructors at Mitkan Adam. Women, who have mandatory two-year stints rather than three, don't serve in Israeli combat units, so they make up over half of the instructor cadre for Special Forces training of the IDF. Most of the sniper instructors at Mitkan Adam were female, for example.

My progress came to a screeching halt at the *Shalishut*—the Administrative Check-in—where I sat on a bench for seven or eight hours, staring at the clock, sweating my balls off. Various officers came over throughout that day, muttering under their breath, glancing at my file, trying to figure out where to send me. I had arrived about three weeks late because of the timing of my *gibush* and the fact that I'd originally tried out for Sayeret Matkal. It was a clusterfuck—nobody knew what to do with me.

Finally, Commander Elad, a seasoned operator who, I learned later, was from Ilan's unit, Duvdevan, came scurrying over.

"Cohen! You're Aaron Cohen? Follow me!"

Elad was one of three commanders who would be assigned to me and the other thirty guys in my group as our instructors for the next six months. Elad quickly filled me in: They were down one or two guys in the training platoons—prospects who'd fallen by the wayside so far—and they wanted me to take up one of those slots. I got all my equipment and my fatigues issued, with Commander Elad rushing me down to the tents so I could join up with my new unit and begin basic training.

On our way to the tents we ran across a diminutive Yemenite, a sergeant major, the most senior NCO on the base. His name was Boaz. It wasn't until a year later that I learned his hero status within Duvdevan, that he'd been shot multiple times in the back during an operation in the territories and been awarded a medal for valor.

"So this is the guy?" Boaz asked Elad. "This is the kid from Los Angeles?"

Now Boaz grabbed me by the arm. I was taken aback by the fact that he knew who I was.

He led me inside a huge tent—actually two 18 x 52-foot general-purpose army tents set up back-to-back—with cots in neat rows. The twenty-eight recruits were scurrying around us. I scanned the rows of cots, piled with bulletproof vests, weapons, and magazines.

The two training platoons were going through what's called *Trom Tiranut*, which roughly translates as "pre-basic training." Under the Israeli Special Forces system, the first month of basic training is a warm-up. The instructors don't fuck you up too much. They want you to adjust to the military mind-set, so the first month is comprised primarily of calisthenics and rudimentary training.

But as it happened, I showed up at Mitkan Adam on the very last day of *Trom Tiranut*. There was a sense in the air that the easy times were over, that the instructors were getting ready to crank up the psychological and physical pace, trying to get the weakest men in the platoons to quit over the coming months of training and bounce them down to the paratroopers or a regular infantry division.

"Everybody stop what you're doing!" Boaz shouted in Hebrew. "Look at me! This kid came all the way from California, from Beverly Hills, to serve in the Israel Defense Forces. This is what it means to sacrifice. Remember that well."

They all stopped doing what they were doing and stared at me, only for an instant, then went back to scurrying around the tent. Everyone seemed too exhausted, too overwhelmed, to make a big deal about my arrival.

I later came to understand why Boaz had made the announcement: he wasn't just singling me out for being such a Johnny Do-Good Soldier-Boy. He was holding me up as a reminder—a throwback to a bygone era—of the spirit of the highly motivated, secular Jewish volunteer, who had formed the backbone of Israel's fighting force since its formative days. By the time I showed at Mitkan Adam, the Special Forces units, indeed the entire culture of the Israel Defense Forces, were undergoing a sea change. The old-school values that I'd read so much about at the Robert Land Academy, the secular, socialist values of the original kibbutznik fighters like Moshe Dayan, were now very much an anachronism. The fierce patriotism of those nonreligious Zionist Ashkenazim—the *Artza Alinu*—singing, hora-dancing, machine-gun-toting farmer-soldiers—had been the driving spirit of the Israeli army and air force from the War of Independence in 1948, through the Six-Day War of 1967 and the Yom Kippur War of 1973.

But in the aftermath of the disastrous 1982 Lebanon invasion (which divided Israeli society much as the Vietnam War divided the United States), and especially following the First Intifada of 1987, the zeal of the average young Israeli for service had all but vanished. More and more the newspapers were filled with stories of draft-age Sabras evading service, traveling abroad, looking for a taste of the good life in Europe and America. And more and more, it was the modern Orthodox kids, the *kippot sruggot*—"knitted yarmulkes," shorthand for the religious Zionists—who took up the call to arms. By the 1990s, the *kippot sruggot* made up a majority of Israel's NCO's and petty officers, and were playing increasingly important roles in Special Forces as well. Rather than the secular nationalism of Israel's founding fathers, the religious values of the young modern Orthodox kids gave them the motivation and commitment level needed to make it through the training.

We didn't realize it when we were busting our asses at Wingate, but that first tryout is almost a joke. The real physical and psychological pain starts at Mitkan Adam. In the United States and European democracies, our instructors' behavior and institutional hazing would be considered sadistic, borderline criminal, an open invitation to class-action lawsuits.

The daily regimen was governed by a kind of Darwinian calculus. Any weakness was pounced on, exploited, punished without pity. From day one, we were reminded constantly that ninety-nine out of one hundred prospects would be sent home. To survive, we had to become emotionless automatons, pure fighting machines. The instructors were breaking us down to a blank slate, reconditioning us from top to bottom: mind, body, and spirit.

Those first few weeks of basic training flew past in a blur: nonstop running, hours on the rifle range, shooting hundreds of rounds, being timed at everything. We were sprinting back and forth to every location. We weren't allowed to walk, or take a breather, even when we were in the kitchen, washing dishes. Everything was to be done double-time. We were being screamed at constantly.

Don't be a big shot, I would tell myself constantly. *Just be in the middle. Don't rise. Don't talk. Don't get your name called out. Don't be too good. Don't be too bad. Just float in the middle.*

Float in the middle. That was my goal, my military mantra, for the next year and half. There was barely time to make friends during basic training, though a couple of recruits and I later became close when we served together in the unit. One guy was named Inon; after our three years together, he went on to serve as an officer in the unit, and today he's still working for Israel's Department of Defense.

Inon wasn't American-born, but he might as well have been. He was a rich-kid Sabra who grew up in the city of Savyon, a northern suburb of Tel Aviv, a mini Beverly Hills, where a lot of ex-generals and politicians live.

Inon and I jelled pretty quickly, largely because he spoke perfect English. He started helping me translate a lot of written material from Hebrew to English since even routine things like maps and the weapons layout (all the parts were labeled in Hebrew) were still a huge challenge for me.

"How'd you learn such good English, bro?" I asked him one afternoon, after hearing his American accent.

"I lived in Miami for a few years with my folks."

"Funny, I lived in Miami as a kid, too," I said.

We started swapping Florida stories and addresses and Inon told me he'd bounced around a lot as a kid between homes in Miami and Tel Aviv.

He was square-jawed, with dark brown eyes, stood about five ten, slim, well built, of Sephardic descent. I went to his house in Savyon a few times on the weekend and we used to hang out at the beach. Inon was the one true star in the unit. He had "it" and everyone could tell. From day one, he glided through every assignment and challenge. And it wasn't just physical prowess. He excelled because of his personality, because he was so honest, humble, and direct.

People assume that to stand out in Special Forces training you must be a physical beast, but honesty and integrity are actually the two most important qualities that the instructors look for. You can teach someone how to shoot correctly; you can teach him the correct three-point stance with an M-4 or an Uzi; you can teach him how to rappel flawlessly into a window. But you can't teach him how to have internal strength, to have moral values and core decency.

It took me a long time to realize that was what the instructors were evaluating. Were you honorable? Were you humble? Were you a *mensch*? If you were ordered to carry a bucket of water from Point A to Point B sixteen times a day, would you keep doing it, even when the instructors' backs were turned, just because you'd been ordered to do it sixteen times? Did you have the integrity and backbone to stand shoulder-to-shoulder with your brothers no matter what the risks?

Shimon Peres, later to serve as prime minister, but defense minister during the legendary Raid on Entebbe, put it well in regard to Matkal, but the ethic holds for all the Special Forces in Israel.

> The unit is based on humility, which has to do with the nature of its activity, and on modesty, which reflects the character of its men. Woe to the one who speaks an unnecessary word or displays even a hint of bravado. Yoni [Netanyahu] insisted on this. He used

to say to his men, "I believe that the danger in the life of the unit is to allow ourselves to become smug. I would like the men in the battalion to always feel a bit worried that there is something else we could have done, that we could have improved upon."

—Shimon Peres, former Israeli prime minister

There was one kid in our platoon who didn't have it. His name was Shai. Like Inon, Shai was a Sabra who spoke perfect English. He was over six feet tall, as blond and blue-eyed as a Norwegian or Swede. Of all of us, he might have been the most fit; he was an animal physically. But he worked out his mouth more than any other muscle in his body! It was all about ego with him.

He'd pull some posturing, look-at-me bullshit, and the instructors would ridicule him for how seriously he took himself. He would find himself in some minor position of power—the deputy in charge of the platoon, for example, making sure that we were sticking to the training schedule—and he would invariably give off an air of presumption and egotism, chest puffed out, as if he were naturally the most qualified among us to be placed in a leadership role.

Massive mistake. The instructors proceeded to rip him apart.

"You've been here for three months," one of the instructors sneered. "Shut your fucking mouth, asshole! Just do what we tell you to do and don't play the big shot!"

He made the cardinal error of basic training: he tried to stand out by being *too* good. It backfired. By the second month, the instructors were leveling him on a daily basis. Shai was constantly doing punishment push-ups, running up hills, being screamed at. The instructors doled out such a level of verbal, physical, and psychological abuse that finally, sometime in our third month, Shai quit.

"I'm getting the fuck out of here," he muttered to us. "I'm going to a different unit. I can't handle this." And he ended up getting himself assigned to a regular infantry unit. I never saw Shai again.

Everyone in basic training at Mitkan Adam knew we'd been preselected for a Special Forces unit, but we didn't talk about it. We didn't dare speculate, think aloud, or ask the instructors how they thought we were doing. Each one of us was fighting for survival, and since we weren't even close to success yet, there was no sense talking about it.

Every training battalion was made up of different units, some destined to be elite Special Forces, others bound for a variety of regular army units where they would wind up working not-too-glamorous stints at checkpoints, driving trucks, or attached to tank units. The selection process was so varied that a major gulf developed between the volunteers who were gung-ho to be in Special Forces and the conscripts who didn't even want to be in the Army.

We had one platoon in our battalion that was nearly 100 percent-gold-chain-wearing Sephardic homeboys from rough neighborhoods—the derisive slang in Hebrew is *arsim*, from the Arabic word for "pimps"—who were forced to serve in combat units because they had the physical stature. But they hated being in uniform. They knew they would ultimately be in a mechanized infantry platoon attached to a tank battalion—a fairly low-status but high-risk unit within the IDF—and they kept doing everything they could to get themselves dropped from training, even if it meant getting sent to jail.

These *arsim* were constantly going to the brig for simple disobedience, ignoring direct orders, not getting out of bed for morning formation. In Israel, military jail isn't such a big deal. They lock you up for a few weeks, the military judge bawls you out, then you come back to the Army.

We often had midnight inspections. All the units in our battalion would be in formation—in Israel, there's no starching and pressing of uniforms, so you just make sure that you've cleaned your guns and laid out your ammo and gear in order. The sergeant would stroll through the formations: Our unit—perfect. Another unit of potential Shaldag commandos—perfect. And then right next to us, there'd be this half-assed Sephardic unit falling apart, disheveled, grumbling, doing everything they could *not* to look perfect.

Our sergeant would ream us out, make us do push-ups, known in the IDF as the "second position," or *matzav shtayim*, over the slightest mistake.

"Matzav shtayim!" our sergeant would scream at us.

The Sephardic kids would howl with laughter.

It may sound illogical to throw elite volunteers in alongside unmotivated conscripts, but there is method in the madness. The commanders mix the undisciplined guys in with the Special Forces trainees to inspire them, and for us, I guess, to see them as a negative example. And it works. The mixture functions as an effective social leveler.

The next several months were spent getting us qualled up to the basic infantry and advanced infantry level. On the one hand, the instructors were doing everything they could to get us to quit, but Israel is such a tiny country it doesn't have the luxury of losing too much time or too many resources. Even if you do get thrown out of the Special Forces training, you're at least qualified to serve in the paratroopers or another regular army unit.

We fired countless rounds with the long-barreled M-16, a big, ugly rifle disparagingly known as the "broomstick." We studied camouflage, fieldcraft, elementary navigation. This was the crash course in basic infantry work, how to kick ass and take land in the event that Israel is attacked—as it has been, virtually every decade—by its Arab neighbors.

Over those first months, we began to jell as a unit. Our instructors were veteran soldiers from the unit and they were in charge of evaluating us, deciding who would be right for which units as well as drilling us in all the basics. It comes down to shekels, plain and simple. They have a limited amount of time to figure out who's worth spending money on. And the dropout rate is phenomenally high. We lost at least one-third of the recruits we started with.

Other veteran operators, ultra-cocky in their red berets and handguns, would come rolling through Mitkan Adam from time to time, dropping off weapons and ammo or coming to teach specific lessons. One morning, I thought I caught a quick glimpse of Ilan, but I didn't dare make eye contact. We couldn't help but notice the tinted-window Savannahs, Yukons, and Ford vans, all tricked out with supercharged V8 engines and Level 7 body armor, but we were supposed to act like they were a desert mirage. One guy made the mistake of looking over at the vans, stealing a glance while we were in formation. The instructors swarmed him, screaming: "You haven't even earned the right to *listen* to that van's engine, never mind *look* at it!"

The kid was shattered, his facial muscles twitching in fear.

The fact that this was an all-volunteer unit meant that anyone could quit at any time. It also meant that anyone could be *dropped* at any time. Once every three weeks, before we went off on a three-day leave, we did what's called *socio-meter,* which derived from the term "sociological meter," but which we used to call the "asshole check." Everyone sat around the tent in total silence, barely making eye contact with one another. We were all handed little scraps of paper. We scribbled a name, then dropped the name into the hat.

Nobody knew who dropped which name. The process was supposed to be completely anonymous. Only the commanders went through the slips of paper, abruptly telling one unlucky guy that it was time to pack his shit and move out. Sometimes the choice was a surprise to everyone but, more often than not, we all knew which way the wind is blowing. A few instructors walked up to me on the sly, while I was crossing the training compound, and whispered, "What do you think of so-and-so over here?"

And, I'd say, "In all honesty, I think he's a total prick," or, "He's a jerk—acts like his shit don't stink."

"Yeah, well, let's see what happens. You never know. He might be gone next week."

NINE

Throughout basic training, instructors engaged in a brutal level of harassment, as unrelenting as a hailstorm. They would tell us over and over: *We don't want you here; we don't need you there.* During every drill and task, there would be an officer, a sergeant, and two commanders, watching our every move. With the exception of the officer, they put every ounce of energy and creativity they could muster into breaking us down. The physical torment was bad enough; the psychological pressure was even harder to deal with. Constant needling, taunting, unlike anything I'd ever experienced. On top of whatever physical pain I was dealing with, I'd have some sergeant whispering like a gnat my ear: "So you want to quit? You want to quit? Maybe it's just not for you. It's not for everybody. Paratroopers is also a good unit. You could drop out and join the paratroopers. You still get the red beret, you still get red boots. If you want to be somewhere else, fine, just tell me now. You're history, gone, simple as that . . ."

Over the years, several young men have died in Special Forces training, simply because the instructors were intent on having the new volunteers experience the same brutal training that *they* had to endure in their time. Not too long ago, for example, a trainee died from severe dehydration. Military hearings were held, jail sentences were meted out to the instructors and commanders, and the Special Forces were required to scale back the level of abuse the instructors are allowed to engage in.

It wasn't always the instructors' fault. More often than not, our own motivation to succeed drove us to take chances we shouldn't have. And sometimes it was hard to tell who was to blame. At some point during basic training, every single one of us was near the edge, hanging on by a thread, on the verge of breaking down physically and mentally.

I lost my composure once in the field, and I thought that was the end of the line for me, that I was about to be shipped out to some random infantry unit to finish up my three years. Every guy in the unit has a similar story to tell. For me, it happened during what's called "War Week," around the fifth month of training, during which the instructors took us out into the desert for the closest possible simulation of wartime conditions.

We lived in a trench for seven straight days, wearing the same uniform all week, the same stinking underwear, socks, and boots. By the fourth or fifth day, we were not only miserable, we were starting to get delirious from lack of sleep.

The only good thing I'd discovered in basic training was a newfound appreciation for sleep. You actually retrain your body to maximize whatever sleep you get. When I sacked out for five hours, my eyes were closed for exactly 300 minutes. No tossing and turning, no waking up in the middle of the night to piss—I don't even remember dreaming once while I was in the Army. I would close my eyes at lights out and, boom, open them at reveille. We'd train mercilessly for three weeks solid, then get a single weekend leave. Everyone headed home to sleep for twenty-six or twenty-seven hours, straight hours. My body completely shut down, experiencing a kind of short-term hibernation in which it could recharge its battery after all that sprinting, forced marches, and trench-digging. Eventually, my body adjusted to the tempo, and I could function for about four days on next to no sleep. But that took a long time to learn. Sleep deprivation was one of the hardest aspects of army life and it reached its peak during War Week. Legally the instructors were only required to give us three or four hours of sleep a night. You start to get buggy, almost hallucinatory, especially in that desert heat. We were putting in twenty-hour days, digging holes and practicing combat maneuvers—nonstop movement—during which any fuckup was punished by making us run up hills or do push-ups until our muscles screamed for mercy.

They kept moving us around from place to place. We'd spend twelve hours in one camp, sleeping perhaps two, then we would train ferociously for eighteen hours, then move to another camp and sleep for another hour. The army knows that sleep deprivation is dangerous territory, so they triple the number of instructors per platoon, just to keep a closer eye on us.

By day four of War Week, we were all getting delusional. I felt like I was tripping on LSD: there's a point where sleeplessness leads to a kind of disembodied, floating euphoria, when you start seeing visions, oversized lizards and biblical ghosts in the desert shadows. That day, in the middle of an instructional lecture, our sergeant stooped down, plucked something from the ground, and started waxing philosophical.

"This is interesting," he said. "Does anyone know what this is? Does anyone know what species of flower I'm holding?"

My God! It was such a random comment, muttering about some tiny pink desert flower growing in the middle of nowhere. No one in the platoon had a clue what he was talking about. Then he raised his voice sternly to a command.

"There are twenty guys here! Someone should be able to figure out what kind of flower this is."

Some murmuring in the ranks, but still no one could come up with answer.

"If I don't start hearing answers in the next ten seconds, then this platoon is going to pick up every single flower in the entire region," he shouted.

The sergeant must have caught something in my expression because, in the next instant, he was pointing his long index finger directly at me.

"Aaron, you look like you have something to say. Can you tell me what type of flower this is?"

I stared at him, in pure defiance, and spoke to him in English. It was the first time during basic training that I'd spoken to any of the instructors in English.

"Who gives a *fuck* what type of flower this is? We haven't slept in *four* days!"

"Aaron?" he said, in a mocking whisper. "What happened? *Nishbarta*? You broke?"

Suddenly, all of the instructors converged on me, surrounded me, like white blood cells forming around an infection. They were all in my face, gazing intently, hovering, ready to strike, waiting for me to give them the pretext to kick me out of the unit.

And the recruits next to me were whispering: "Aaron, shut the fuck up. Shut up, shut up, shut up. Don't talk back."

I was on the borderline. I felt so close to cracking, smelling the instructors' hot, angry breath in my face. I was ready to tell them to go fuck themselves and send me off to whatever mechanized infantry or tank battalion they saw fit. But then I pulled it together, breathing deeply, reminding myself how badly I wanted to succeed, to make it into the ranks of a Special Forces unit.

I've since run similar training exercises; I know today what the instructor was doing. He didn't give a damn about the name of the flower. Being an elite IDF Special Forces soldier is not about being the fastest runner or the straightest shooter. The sole purpose of the flower-naming exercise was to add more stress and annoyance and harassment, to see if this minor and inconsequential task would be the straw that broke one of our backs. That entire week of hell was teaching us to work as a unit under a high degree of emotional pressure, with practically no sleep, while performing various tasks in timed intervals. It's as close as they can come to simulating the stress and pressure of wartime conditions.

They took me out of formation, led me to a hill, and ordered me to start crawling. I crawled over rocky, thorny desert terrain for hours. I still have the scars on my forearms to prove it.

And the punishment didn't end when the sun set. Later that night, they pulled me out of the tent along with another recruit named Adi, who'd always been the slowest crawler. They took us back to that hill, three stories high with a seventy-degree gradient. One of the instructors planted his little fluorescent stick on the top of the hill, and every time he shouted "Go!" we had to crawl to the fluorescent light, do a tight U-turn, and crawl back down. It was a two-minute crawl up, and a two-minute crawl down, and just to be extra-sadistic, they chose a path with the most cactuses and thorns.

For hours, in the pitch black, we crawled up that goddamned hill, blood seeping through my ripped fatigues. The instructors were laughing at us. "Get up the hill, you lazy fucks!"

I heard myself screaming back at them. "You're not going to get me to fucking quit. Fuck it! I'll crawl all year if I have to!"

At last, Adi couldn't take the pain anymore. I heard a quiet little voice in the darkness next to me, halfway between a whisper and a groan, say: "Fuck. I'm done."

But there was no easy way out—for either of us. As soon Adi said he was quitting, the commander stood over us screaming at the top of his lungs.

"Cohen! If Adi doesn't finish, we're throwing *you* out!"

That's the kind of twisted mind game they play. I knew there was no way I was going to encourage or psyche Adi into crawling up the hill again. But the commander wasn't giving either one of us a break.

"You bring him up the fucking hill, bring him around the fluorescent light, and bring him back down with you! I don't care how it happens! Make it happen! Get off your ass, Aaron!"

Adi, meanwhile, was practically in tears, fighting me off. "Don't touch me! Leave me the fuck alone!"

I had to haul him up and back, through the thorns and cactuses, even though he was fighting me tooth and nail. At last I heard the commander telling me to stop.

"Aaron, stand up."

"I can't move, sir."

All four instructors grabbed their canteens and started dumping cold water on me.

They let Adi have his way, too. They transferred him out of the unit at first light.

TEN

At the seven-month mark, the regular combat units in the battalion had a big celebration. They had made it through the worst. But the Special Forces training units had no ceremony, no recognition, not even a pat on the back.

"We've got another fucking eight months left," we all said to each other. "This is just the beginning of the shit-storm."

We received one major status symbol when we were issued our short-barreled M-16s, a compact, maneuverable weapon primarily used for urban counterterrorism missions—as opposed to the long M-16 used by infantry combat units. Then we got a week off to rest. By this time, I'd rented a one-bedroom apartment at 7 Hannah Senesh in Tel Aviv for my weekend leaves. I spent that week catching up on my sleep, drinking a few beers, riding my motorcycle, and hanging out with Inon at the beach.

And I took my short M-16 around with me everywhere. It was like a trophy; I wasn't about to put it down for a minute. People in restaurants and cafés were staring, smiling, mocking me—in Israeli society, they think you're a loser if you act too gung-ho about your army service—but I didn't give a fuck. I was so proud of how far I'd managed to come that I carried that gun everywhere like it was attached to my body.

Seven days later we had our game faces back on. We met at Reading, the main bus station pickup for soldiers who are in the pipeline for the combat units as well as for Special Forces. Reading is located at a none-too-picturesque spot on the Mediterranean, at the northern part of the beachfront, where huge smokestacks tower over the suburbs of Tel Aviv.

When we showed up, we saw rows and rows of *tiholit*, or special buses, to transport soldiers to and from each base. The headquarters of our unit—by this time, we all realized we were bound for the "cherry unit," Duvdevan—is one of the most-classified bases in the entire Central Command, and for obvious security reasons, I can't be too specific about the location. I won't even give the Duvdevan base its actual name; let's call it Machanet Gibor—Hebrew for *hero*. The most interesting fact about Machanet Gibor is this: the base is hidden in plain view, just outside a major Palestinian city on the West Bank, which means it's a hub of counterterrorism operations located right in the heart of the Occupied Territories.

The security perimeter around the base is severe. Along the drive, we passed various checkpoints, patrols and armed guards with their handheld radios constantly squawking. For most of us, this was the first time any of us had entered the territories in our careers.

From the exterior, nothing about Machanet Gibor indicates that it is a top-secret military base. On the contrary, the facade is a perfect fabrication of a Palestinian street scene, consisting of shambling houses, huts, and storefronts, meandering goats, old men dressed in galabias and keffiyehs. There's even a mosque, whose gleaming dome can be seen from a distance.

Our bus stopped by a concrete wall and two uniformed soldiers, armed with M-16s, approached the driver.

Beyond that faux Palestinian shantytown lies a sprawling military compound, with barracks, firing ranges, and state-of-the-art SUVs, jeeps, and other military vehicles parked over several acres. We were waved onto the base, piled out of the bus, and assigned to quarters, since trainees have extremely limited access around the base. We were largely confined to one corner of the facility for the first six months.

They led us to an open field where we assembled in standard formation, a three-sided square called a *chet* (for the eighth letter of the Hebrew alphabet). Our instructors from Mitkan Adam walked onto the field along with two or three new instructors we'd never seen before. They'd all shed their red boots and berets; most were bareheaded, wearing New Balance sneakers, 9-mm Sig Sauer handguns holstered on their hips.

Though the dress code was more relaxed, the training regimen was anything but. As soon as we took our places in our *chet* formation, the team of instructors converged, pacing in front of us. I recognized Ilan Rubenstein immediately. It was the first time I'd seen Ilan up close since that day at Wingate. But he didn't offer me so much as a nod. His demeanor was pure hard-ass. Still, I felt a surge of relief, knowing I'd made it far enough to find myself under his direct training for Duvdevan.

"Listen up!" Ilan shouted. "Everything that we were not allowed to do to you at Mitkan Adam for legal reasons, *that's* what we're going to do to you here."

Everybody shit an onion. Our bodies were smoked from the last six months, but we could all see that Ilan was dead serious.

For the first time, we began to understand what it was like to be trained for a unit unlike any other in the entire Israel Defense Forces: an elite "Arabist" counterterrorism unit, charged with undertaking lightning-quick response missions in the West Bank, often, though not always, utilizing sophisticated undercover techniques of *mista'aravim*.

We broke ranks and the instructors explained that the focus of the next two months would be acquiring the essential skills Duvdevan employs in the field. Training would be a lot less about mind games and a lot more tactical. We would learn the core operational skills to function as a professional counterterrorism team.

We started by learning the basics of navigation. In Hebrew, these lessons are known as *Topo* (for *topografia*), meaning open-field navigation, and *Tatza* (an acronym for *tzlumat avir*), meaning navigation in an urban environment from aerial and satellite imagery.

During *Topo*, we worked primarily in sprawling desert terrain with mountain ranges and foothills, reading details as minute as bushes and trees.During *Tatza* we were dropped off in various Palestinian or primarily Arab cities like Jaffa within Israel's borders, and ordered to complete a variety of navigational tasks based solely on aerial photographs from satellites.

We quickly learned how difficult it is to get your bearings from such scant information in a densely populated city or town. We struggled to read the jagged streets and walls and other landmarks in order to navigate our way home. Yet over time we each mastered the art of reading such photographs, breaking them down the way we would any other map and triangulating ourselves from three different points on the photograph.

In essence, we were learning to do what bombardiers did during World War II missions, the only difference being that *we* were the bombs. We would not be dropping explosives on a target from high altitudes; we'd be putting ourselves and our teammates inside the apartment complex, the mosque, or the training compound.

We worked closely with Israeli intelligence, downloading images from satellites, planes, and drones—anywhere we could get them. Duvdevan never relies on someone else's outdated photograph, even if it's just a few weeks old. Things change too rapidly in an urban setting, especially in the territories. The terrorists we hunted were constantly on the move, always changing safe houses. Consequently, we developed brand-new photographic imagery, even en route to a mission. Images straight from satellites would print out right in our camouflaged vans. We might have had orders to take down a target at a certain location only to learn, minutes from our destination, that he might be in one of four houses. Or we might have gotten fresh intel to expand the mission from our original target to his uncle down the block, or in the adjacent neighborhood.

Without the bedrock training in urban and open-field topographical navigation, we could never hope to be effective operators going out on life-and-death missions in the territories.

For me, one of the most exciting moments was Ilan's announcement that we were beginning basic counterterrorism (or C.T.) training. Duvdevan is the only pure counterterrorism unit in Israel: our mission isn't reconnaissance, border patrol, or advanced infantry—we are trained in all three, but that's not our mandate. Our single focus is to undertake stealth counterterrorism operations in the Occupied Territories. This means our final eight months of training before becoming operational are devoted *exclusively* to mastering the most advanced counterterrorism tactics ever devised.

We started our counterterrorism training with short-barreled M-16 work. Over the decades, this light, compact, lethal weapon has become the standard tool of most commando and counterterrorist operations. To use them in an urban environment, we learned a completely different way to hold the gun, a different way to stand. We were no longer falling to the ground and squeezing off rounds from the prone position used by typical infantrymen. We were learning how to handle a submachine gun while breaking down doors and engaging in house-to-house fighting where every bystander might be a potential combatant and things can change at lightning speed.

The instructors were remolding us, teaching us to shoot standing up, keeping the weapon tight to our bodies, showing us all the urban weapon tactics that Israelis have perfected over the decades, working specifically in dense, built-up urban areas.

At last I felt like I could see the light at the end of the tunnel, that the previous ten months of abuse and testing had been for a greater purpose. We were training our minds as well as our bodies and the professional skills we were learning would ultimately stop and prevent acts of terror in the future.

ELEVEN

We were now given the luxury of six hours' sack time, the other eighteen hours were spent perfecting our urban M-16 work and heading out on the bus each day to continue our navigation drills in pairs. During the bus ride, we were not allowed to sleep, daydream, or relax. On every trip, the instructors institute what they call "aggressiveness training," which entails making every man fight tooth-and-nail up and down the length of the bus, a brutal exercise designed to get us over the natural human fear of being hit. We were already dog-tired after putting in long days in the field, and the moment we piled onto the bus, Ilan or one of the other instructors would start shouting: "Whoever's sitting in seat Number 20, I want him to get over to seat Number 3—now! Nobody lets him get there!"

It became like "King of the Ring," minus any sense of fun. Pure mayhem, a free-for-all, getting your head kicked in by forty guys at a time. It was a two-hour ride back to the base and we did aggressiveness training nonstop. And, God forbid, we fucked up and let one of the guys slip through to the seat. The instructors would immediately stop the bus, order everybody off, and make us sprint forty meters between the rocks and trees.

Oddly enough, there was an upside. After months of close quarters and constant stress and competitiveness, it's only natural that you develop some pet peeves and resentments. My own level of pent-up frustration was off the charts. The daily navigation drills were especially hard for me, given that my Hebrew was still rudimentary, and we had to read very detailed maps with the names printed in minute typeface. So I actually enjoyed the aggressiveness training. It gave me the chance to beat the shit out of everyone who'd been getting under my skin for months.

Nevertheless, it was a primal and oftentimes frightening thing to experience. For a few hours each day, we turned into a pack of animals, like wild dogs fighting over a scrap of meat. To avoid the risk of doing permanent damage, we weren't allowed to hit each other in the face or head, so there was a constant barrage of kidney and gut shots and periodic body slams to the floor. A lot of fingers and ribs got fractured during the two months on that stupid bus. But more important, making a man fight his way through thirty or forty other men every day for two months changes him in a profound psychological way. It hardwires a brand of aggression that becomes impossible to turn off. Later, even when I was on leave, I would walk through crowded shopping malls in Tel Aviv and, if a bunch of random teenagers blocked my path, I'd just start to elbow and body-check them out of my way without a second thought. It's a mind-set that has never gone away either, even once I left the army. That aggressiveness training gets inside your mental circuitry and alters you forever.

To balance the wild aggression of the bus drill, we began basic Krav Maga at night, each class lasting about three or four hours in the gymnasium. Krav Maga, which basically translates as "full-contact fighting," is a self-defense system and martial art developed primarily in Israel but which has, in recent years, become increasingly popular with military and police forces around the world. Krav Maga was the brainchild of Budapest-born Imi Lichtenfeld, a former boxer and wrestler who developed his system in Bratislava in the mid-1930s in order to help protect the Jewish community from attacks by Nazi thugs. Upon arriving in the British Mandate of Palestine, Lichtenfeld began teaching his weaponless combat system to the Haganah, and after the War of Independence, he became the chief instructor of physical fitness and Krav Maga at the IDF's School of Combat Fitness. Little celebrated outside Israel, Lichtenfeld's legacy is a "real-world" fighting system—unlike traditional Asian martial arts like karate, kung fu, or Muay Thai, there's no sport variation of Krav Maga—whose philosophy is built on several simple, effective principles:

Do as much damage as quickly as possible.

Immediately attack your opponent's vulnerable points—eyes, throat, groin, solar plexus.

Transition from defense to attack as quickly possible.

Convert any available items into weapons.

Be constantly aware of everything that is unfolding around you.

We always started on the ground, doing knuckle push-ups, to harden our fists, while the Krav instructor talked:

"Every time we give you a Krav lesson, we want 110 percent. There's no defense. When we tell you to attack, you do nothing but attack. When we give you a technique, you use only that technique and you punch until you've got nothing left."

It was a cumulative learning process: Every day we added a new skill, as we learned the basics of what are called the *kravot*—"the combatives." We started off with an hour of bag-work, not too different from traditional boxing or kickboxing. "Now we want a left jab," the instructor would say, and for the next minute or so you threw nothing but left jabs. Then they would add a right cross, an uppercut, a left hook, some elbows, some knees. Then they'd order us into this demonic *shesh al shesh* drill, requiring us to sprint back and forth to the punching bags, touch the wall, back to the bags, ten or twelve times until we were completely winded.

And then, just to mix things up, they'd throw in a variation on our aggressiveness training. They called it Death Row.

"Everybody form a straight line," the Krav instructor would bark. "The first person in the line has to get to the back of the line, but nobody lets him get through, okay? If anyone makes it to the end of the line, trust me, you'll all be sorry."

Through a blur of punches, kicks, and flying knees, the instructor screamed his encouragement:

Israeli passport, issued near the end of my IDF service before I headed back to the United States.

This is the official Duvedan/Unit 217 unit insignia. The logo is composed of four parts: an anchor, a sword, paratrooper wings, and the Israeli intelligence logo. The material on the back of the pin symbolizes the status of warrior: one who has completed all of the mandatory training. Sayeret Matkal and Sayeret Duvdevan were the only units not required to wear any insignia.

Miktan Adam, one of the final shooting ranges where I was tested. In this mock-up of a generic West Bank village, we had to engage multiple targets at varying distances, in a heavily populated area.

During undercover training, dressed in a galabia (the long, flowing robe), with a keffiyeh (the checkered scarf), carrying an AK-47 Kalashnikov, known in Israel as the "Kalatch."

With my candy-apple red Suzuki RF600 in front of my tiny apartment in Tel Aviv.

Striking a pose in front of the Israeli flag, which hung in our tent at Miktan Adam.

Ilan and other members of the unit gearing up for an undercover operation in the territories.

The logo for the Counter Terror School at Miktan Adam—a fierce-looking alley cat with bat wings on its shoulders, an image representing the cunning, stealth, adaptability, and nighttime predatory power that Israeli counterterrorism forces use in the field.

With an RPG, or rocket-propelled grenade launcher, during my stint instructing new trainees.

Ilan, in my room in the unit—as always, with a cigarette and a bottle of Coke.

On Banana Beach, Tel Aviv, on a forty-eight-hour leave from the unit, unwinding from the stress of operational work with some friends, among them Ilan *(back row, right)* and Tal *(back row, left)*.

With Danny Yatom, former general of the Central Command, commander of Sayeret Matkal and former Mossad chief. When I served, top intelligence officers were everywhere; they enjoyed having young warriors around.

With several former members of my unit, disguised as Palestinian Arabs. They're now all members of IMS.

"When I say don't let him through, I mean, *don't let him through*! I don't mean try your best! I mean *don't* let him through! No excuses!"

After one of our more grueling Krav sessions, a stranger appeared in the gym. He was dark-haired, Sephardic, about thirty-six years old. He stood no more than five foot six and weighed about 160 pounds, wearing rumpled fatigues, and had a five o'clock shadow. He didn't strike me as particularly intimidating. The instructor called for another bout of Death Row, and within thirty seconds, using nothing but willpower and his low center of gravity, this tiny guy knocked us all to hell. There was no way we could stop him; we would have had to put a bulldozer in front of him. He was mentally too strong.

After he knocked us on our asses, he promptly left the gym without saying a word. We were speechless, out of breath, grunting in pain.

"Who the fuck was that?" I said.

The instructor wouldn't tell us. But a few weeks later I learned who the little badass was. He was a full colonel named Muki, the commander of the unit.

In order to survive the Krav Maga and aggressiveness drills, you have to become the most hardened of human fighting machines. Still, no amount of toughness—mental or otherwise—can prepare you for the hell of the weekly forced marches.

They didn't seem too daunting at first. The instructors began capping off the week with a forced march, in full uniform with all our weapons and gear. The first one was ten kilometers, through the desert, in the afternoon blaze. I muscled through it, thinking the worst factor to cope with was the heat and my unquenchable thirst. The next march was slightly longer, fifteen kilometers. Then seventeen. Then twenty.

Even as the distances increased, the pace remained intense, never less than a light trot. But by this point our bodies were so well conditioned that we could rattle off a twenty-kilometer hike in the field without too much strain.

Then the commanders ramped it up to forty kilometers, through the scorching desert, past the towering white cliffs of Masada, and we all thought we had reached our bodies' limit for pain.

But we were nowhere *near* our bodies' limit for pain.

No one tells you what you're in for, but you hear it whispered, from the first days of basic training, that if you're one of the "lucky" ones who survive the weeding-out process, you'll have to complete the ultimate physical challenge: the 120-kilometer march, the final hurdle before being awarded the coveted red beret worn only by the Special Forces and select elite units within the IDF.

In Hebrew it's known as *massa kumta*—literally, "the forced march of the beret." From Tel Aviv to Jerusalem, it is 120 kilometers, 90 miles, while your spine is buckling under the weight of fifty pounds of munitions and field equipment.

Because my Hebrew skills were the weakest, the instructors ordered me to carry the platoon radio—a typically sardonic touch of Israeli humor to designate the kid with the biggest language barrier as the "communications" man—which weighed a good thirty pounds, plus my rifle, ammunition, and pack.

Most men probably lose ten pounds in sweat during the march.

We were instructed to hydrate roughly every three kilometers, but we were never allowed to stop moving, even while we lifted our canteens to our parched lips.

Many critics say that the *massa kumta* is outdated, a macho throwback to Israel's formative frontier days, completely irrelevant in today's high-tech military. But psychologically, it remains an enormously important accomplishment—when you can march for twenty-three hours straight, moving between a brisk walk and a light jog the entire time, with sixty to seventy pounds of gear strapped to your back, you're going to develop an enormous reservoir of confidence and self-respect, precisely the kinds of inner qualities you need to be an effective counterterrorism operator.

Twelve hours in, the heat was like a noose tightening around my neck. I could feel my ankles ballooning and blisters erupting on my heels. I remembered the Krav Maga lessons and the way Colonel Muki muscled through ten bigger, stronger, and younger soldiers using mental discipline, focus, and will. Somehow, that image gave me the strength to keep my boots in forward motion.

I kept telling myself that the big prize awaited me at the end, that Colonel Muki and Ilan, and even the brass from the General Command would be at the finish line to greet us and present us with the coveted red berets. We would be treated to an outdoor feast, toasted with wine and song, and welcomed into the brotherhood.

It was somewhere under the parched desert cliffs that I felt myself sliding into delirium. I was thinking about the ancient fortress of Masada, where two millennia ago Jewish zealots committed mass suicide rather than surrender to the Romans. I started to hallucinate. I saw shapes in the desert: bony black demons and red-skinned lizards hissing fire. My feet were turning to hamburger, my brain to mush. I was talking to myself, screaming at myself, coaching myself to stay sane.

They later told I made it to the end of the march, that the commanders of Duvdevan presented me with my red beret. But I have no memory of the ceremony. Because shortly after crossing the finish line, I collapsed unconscious. My dehydration was so severe that I remained hospitalized, with a high fever, on an IV drip for nearly a week while the rest of my team recovered back at the base. The military doctor who treated me said I was lucky. My kidneys were shutting down, going into renal failure. Another hour or two in the desert, he said, and I'd have been a corpse.

TWELVE

After the *massa kumta* we were granted a week off. I wanted to go visit Golda—God knows, I could have used some of her Jewish-grandmother treatment—but I found I could barely leave my little overheated flat at 7 Hannah Senesh. My feet were throbbing, covered in bleeding, oozing blisters. I couldn't walk for the first two days.

While part of me was savoring the feeling of extraordinary accomplishment, I knew the march was only the beginning of the truly difficult work. In most combat units—in the paratroopers, Golani, and Nahal, for example, the colored beret represents the highest goal you can achieve as a rank-and-file soldier in the Israel Defense Forces. For those units, the forced march is the culmination of their training ordeal. But in Special Forces units like Matkal, Shayetet-13, Shaldag, and Duvdevan, it's just another step in a long, long road. We're not even close to making the final cut. We still have six weeks of the

Counter Terror School, the most esteemed—and feared—course in the entire IDF, and then another six months of *lochem gimmel*, or advanced warrior training, to complete successfully.

Back at Mitkan Adam, I passed for the first time through the doors of the C.T. School, entering under the school's logo: a fierce-looking alley cat with bat wings on its shoulders, an image representing the cunning, stealth, adaptability, and nighttime predatory capabilities with which Israeli counterterrorism is applied in the field.

First, I sat through a background briefing on how and why the C.T. School came into existence. Traditionally, Israel's infantry units and police were responsible for developing their own reconnaissance platoons, units fully capable of executing hostage rescue and SWAT-style terrorist takedowns. But twenty years ago, the General Command decided to put those reconnaissance units through a standardized, intensive Counter Terror School, so that in the event of a hostage situation, the army units closest to the crisis could immediately deploy, acting as an immediate response team, securing and controlling the scene while awaiting the police C.T. unit to arrive. This standardization and coordination in a multilayered system of response was a key philosophical breakthrough in the nation's counterterrorism philosophy. The term in Hebrew is *itarvut*—literally "intervention" but implying immediate response with a high-level counterterrorism capability.

We began a six-week course known as Sha-Dov—an acronym of Shimshon and Duvdevan. (As I said earlier, Sayeret Shimshon, or "Samson," the sister unit to Sayeret Duvdevan, had been deployed in the Gaza Strip; when Gaza was returned to the Palestinian Authority as part of the Oslo Accords, many of the fighters from Shimshon were absorbed into Duvdevan and redeployed in the West Bank.) The longest course in the C.T. School, Sha-Dov covers all manner of *itarvut;* the execution of warrants; working undercover (with a special focus on *mista'aravim*, or adopting Arab disguise); using concealed handguns and submachine guns; shooting from moving vehicles; effecting slow and deliberate clearing of houses.

For the first two weeks, we were on the firing ranges for twelve or fourteen hours a day, shooting a staggering number of rounds, as many as five thousand bullets per soldier per week. The pace was unrelenting. The shooting instructors were the cream of the crop. They taught us an entirely new way of using our firearms, a style unique to the Israeli counterterrorism model. Using the short M-16, mini-Uzi, micro-Uzi, AK-47, and a variety of semiautomatic pistols, we trained in LOZ—an acronym for *lechima tzarah* or "in-fighting"—an extremely expensive, time-consuming training, requiring a great deal of hand-eye coordination, reserved for Special Forces counterterrorism units. We started with single shots, then bursts of two, then three. We couldn't take our time to line up the targets. If we stopped to aim the gun, the instructors would smack us on the back of the head, simulating the duress and pressure of real-world field operations.

After a few days on the range, one of the veteran instructors ordered us to switch our guns to fully automatic.

"This isn't *Rambo*—nobody can hit a target with any accuracy while shooting on fully auto," the instructor said. "That's only in the fucking movies."

But with our improved reaction times, we learned that we could shoot in semi-automatic mode just as rapidly—and far more accurately. We would squeeze off three rounds per second—*bap-bap-*

bap—and each time the bullet traveled exactly where we intended.

After five weeks of LOZ training, my bullets hit the target in a tight two-inch radius every time. I'd mastered firing the short-barreled M-16, the micro- and mini-Uzis, as well as a variety of 9-mm handgun makes: Glock, Sig Sauer, even Soviet handguns that looked like they were World War II vintage. Much of the weaponry is customized for covert C.T. operations. For example, with the micro-Uzi, a submachine gun more accurate than a pistol because of its folding stock, the C.T. School designed a special harness ideal for wearing under a traditional Palestinian dress; if you are going into the field disguised as an Arab woman, the stretchy, flexible nylon harness fits snugly under the armpit. We trained for hour upon hour, flipping up the flowing fabric, whipping out the micro-Uzi, smacking the stock so that it unfolded cleanly, and then putting twenty rounds into three different targets.

The target ranges mimicked real-world scenarios in an urban environment. Typically, the range would feature cutout silhouettes of a dozen women and children with only one terrorist target mixed in. This was meant to simulate a suspect's taking cover in a crowd of civilians. Obviously, we were not allowed to spray shots indiscriminately—do that and you'd be smacked on the head by one of the instructors. They weren't training us to be a gang of rogue mercenaries with blood dripping from our teeth. It was stressed over and over: On a mission, the team must make every effort to avoid collateral casualties. Through constant repetition, our shooting drills on the range trained us to pick the terrorist target from the crowd of innocent bystanders.

There is simply no substitute for the endless repetition of firing thousands of live rounds, developing accurate and selective shooting across various distances, shooting while on the run, moving methodically around barricades and walls. The instructors were re-calibrating our reaction time and muscle memory. It's one of the many ways we were being transformed from civilians into the most formidable counterterrorist operators in the world.

THIRTEEN

Yoni symbolized in his life and battles the preparedness of the army and its high standards. He showed that on the civilian front, where cruelty takes the place of heroism, and the lack of human norms is the norm—even in such a war the battle is not lost. Operation Entebbe, with Yoni at its heart, was the first sign to the world that one must not give in to terror, that it is possible to overcome it.

—Shimon Peres, former Israeli prime minister

When we weren't on the range, we were in the classroom studying the Israeli Special Forces history, analyzing and breaking down the most famous raids, hostage rescues, and counterterrorist missions. We dissected every moment of Operation Thunderbolt (the famed raid at Entebbe); Operation Wrath of God, the raid in which Ehud Barak, the future prime minister, dressed as a woman, led a *mista'aravim* squad in a devastating attack on a Palestinian terrorist cell in Beirut (a mission depicted in Steven Spielberg's *Munich*); Operation Isotope, the 1972 Sabena hijacking in which Barak and Bibi Netanyahu figured prominently (coming through the door during the raid, Netanyahu was shot by friendly fire).

But our history classes weren't one long back-patting session about the sterling successes of the IDF. In fact, we spent more time analyzing the famous failures, where operations went catastrophically wrong, and how Israel adapted its Special Forces training accordingly. A classic example is the Ma'alot massacre of 1974, to this day one of the most traumatic terror acts in the Israeli consciousness.

On May 15, 1974, the twenty-sixth anniversary of Israel's independence, three heavily armed terrorists, members of the Popular Democratic Front for the Liberation of Palestine, stormed into Ma'alot High School in northern Israel, taking several dozen teachers and students hostage and demanding the release of twenty-three Arab and three other prisoners, including Kozo Okamoto—a Japanese man involved in the attack on Lod Airport in 1972. If these demands were not met, they would begin executing the students at six P.M. The Israeli parliament met in an emergency session and by three P.M. they had reached a decision to negotiate, but the PDFLP members refused a request to extend the negotiation period. At the time, there were no designated counterterrorism units in Israel, so it fell on Sayeret Matkal, then the unit with the most advanced C.T. capability, and members of Sayeret Golani, one of the most venerable and decorated outfits in the IDF, to carry out the rescue attempt.

At 5:45 P.M., the team of Matkal and Golani Special Forces stormed the building. They managed to kill all the hostage takers, but not before the terrorists had killed twenty-six Israeli children. Another sixty people were wounded. It was one of the greatest national traumas in Israeli history—perhaps even greater than the murder of the Olympic athletes in Munich in 1972. Funerals were held soon after, with some of the ten thousand mourners chanting "Death to the terrorists!" The public demanded an immediate retaliatory response and the next day the Israeli Air Force bombed seven Palestinian refugee camps and villages in southern Lebanon which they said were being used as training bases by the terrorists, killing 27 people and injuring 138.

In class, we examined over and over again what went wrong during the mission and what could be gleaned from the errors. At the beginning of the raid, a Matkal sniper tried to take out one of the terrorists, who was guarding the hostages, all of whom were dressed in fake IDF uniforms. The sniper, using an old Mauser 98—a weapon no modern C.T. operator would use in such a situation—and not trained in short-range headshot sniping, failed to kill the target. The wounded Palestinian started throwing grenades into the crowd of huddled hostages and spraying them with automatic gunfire.

The Matkal commandos, for all their undeniable bravery, were not trained in the standard counterterrorism techniques we learn today, specific urban tactics like close-quarter battle (or "CQB") pinpoint shooting. In the aftermath of the Ma'alot massacre, reacting to the deafening public outcry, the Israeli government and the IDF General Staff made some important strategic decisions, including the foundation of a new civilian C.T. Unit (later known as Unit Yamam, an acronym of Yechida Meuchedet Mishtartit, or Special

Police Unit), requiring that all of Israel's Special Forces units acquire advanced C.T. capabilities, with Sayeret Matkal and Shayetet-13 on the cutting edge until the formation of the designated *mista'aravim* units in 1987.

Yet no lesson made such an impression on me as the story of the most heroic counterterrorism operation in Israel's—or any other country's—history: the rescue of the hostages at Entebbe Airport in July 1976. I'd read about it countless times since my adolescent days at Robert Land, but learning the specifics of the mission now from actual Israeli Special Forces veterans gave those stories an entirely new, much more profound, resonance.

By the mid-1970s, Israel was reeling from an onslaught of Arab attacks on civilians, from the first (and only) hijacking in July 1968 of an El Al airliner, whose passengers were kept for an excruciating forty days, to the Munich Olympics murders, Sabena Airlines hijacking and Lod Airport attack in 1972, and the Ma'alot massacre two years later. Israel felt boxed into a corner. Its much-heralded military and air force had proven it could defeat the armed forces of the Arab world, but how could Israel combat acts of brazen terrorism directed at unarmed civilians? The nation would either continue to be victimized or it would have to respond with unprecedented boldness.

That was the historical context of the breathtaking rescue mission performed by Sayeret Matkal to free more than one hundred hostages being held at Entebbe Airport in Uganda. On June 27, 1976, Air France Flight 139, which had originated in Tel Aviv, took off from Athens with 248 passengers and a crew of twelve, heading for Paris.

Soon after takeoff, the flight was hijacked by two Palestinians from the Popular Front for the Liberation of Palestine and two German terrorists. They diverted the plane to Benghazi, Libya, where the jet was held on the ground for seven hours for refueling. A female hostage who pretended she was pregnant was released, then the plane left Benghazi. At 3:15 P.M., it arrived at Entebbe Airport in Uganda.

On the ground, the four hijackers were joined by three more Arab guerrillas, supported by Uganda's pro-Palestinian president, Idi Amin. The hijackers demanded the release of forty Palestinians being held in Israel and thirteen other detainees imprisoned in Kenya, France, Switzerland, and Germany, including the Japanese Red Army terrorists responsible for the Lod Airport massacre. If Israel refused to cooperate, they would begin killing hostages on July 1, 1976.

The hijackers corralled the hostages in the old terminal of Entebbe Airport. They released a large number of hostages, keeping only the Israeli nationals and Jews. When he was informed of his impending release, Air France Captain Michel Bacos told the hijackers that all passengers were his responsibility, and that he would not leave any of them. Bacos's entire crew courageously followed suit. A French nun also refused to leave, insisting that one of the Jewish hostages take her place, but she was forced into the waiting Air France airliner—another jet had been flown in specifically for the released hostages—by Ugandan soldiers. A total of eighty-three Israeli and Jewish hostages remained behind, as well as twenty Air France crew members.

As the July 1 deadline approached, the government of Israel, under the leadership of Prime Minister Yitzhak Rabin, offered to negotiate with the hijackers in order to extend the deadline to July 4.

The Israeli cabinet was prepared to release the Palestinian prisoners if a military solution seemed unlikely to succeed. Meanwhile, a retired IDF officer, Baruch "Burka" Bar-Lev, who had known Idi Amin for years, spoke to the Ugandan leader on the phone many times, attempting to negotiate the release of the hostages, without success.

A seemingly impossible rescue mission was hatched when all diplomatic avenues seemed doomed to failure. On July 3, the cabinet approved an unprecedented commando mission under the direction of Major General Yekutiel Adam. For a time, the plan was to dispatch Shayetet-13 commandos who would land in Lake Victoria and approach Entebbe by water in the dead of night. Ultimately, the General Command determined that a more viable plan was an airborne commando mission under the leadership of Sayeret Matkal's commanding officer, Colonel Yonatan "Yoni" Netanyahu, and the overall command of Dan Shomron.

On paper, the rescue attempt made no sense. Shimon Peres later explained the reasoning behind the raid: "In theory, we had no choice. Entebbe was four thousand kilometers [2,500 miles] away from Israel. In theory, there was no military option of saving the hostages. In theory, the terrorists could walk around the airport safely and complacently. Israel could not reach them under the protection of Idi Amin. But only in theory. The Israeli government decided to do the impossible, and initiated a daring operation to free the hostages. It was decided that an airborne task force to Entebbe would land at the airport, break into the building where the hostages were being held, release them, and bring them back to Israel. The operation was entrusted to Yoni."

The raid would take place on the night of July 3 and early morning of July 4, 1976, just as the United States was waking up to celebrate its bicentennial. After days of analyzing the most up-to-the-minute intelligence the Mossad could offer, four Israeli Air Force C-130 Hercules transport aircraft made a stealth flight toward Entebbe Airport, under cover of night, without aid of ground control. They were followed by two Boeing 707 jets. The first Boeing, containing medical supplies and equipment, landed in Nairobi, Kenya, while the other aircraft continued toward Uganda. Shimon Peres recalls the astonishing level of attentiveness that went into the Matkal preparation: "The officers in Yoni's battalion studied their maps the way their forefathers had studied Gemara. Every contour of land, every hidden channel was checked with great care, clarified, explained, and debated to discover any wrinkle, any unfamiliar aspect, any possibility that might be unmarked. Daytime was for the self-indulgent. For these fighters, their field of vision and activity was at night."

The airborne task force was made up of a team of twenty-nine Israel Defense Forces servicemen, primarily members of Sayeret Matkal. The operational plan, devised in less than forty-eight hours, was stunning in its audacity. After the Hercules transports landed, the commandos would brazenly pretend to be Idi Amin and his bodyguard entourage, passing (hopefully) undetected en route to the airport terminal in a motorcade consisting of one tinted-window Mercedes-Benz sedan and Land-Rovers festooned with Ugandan flags. Shimon Peres recalls one particularly famous detail of the mission, the legendary last-second commandeering of a civilian's Mercedes:

> On Friday, a day before the operation, we learned that Idi Amin, who had been outside the country, was about to return on Saturday night, perhaps at the same time that the operation was to

> begin. The boys decided to create their own Idi Amin. "Our" Idi Amin, it was decided, would travel in the newest, most expensive Mercedes limo. A check on the computer revealed which Mercedes cars could be found in Israel. A vehicle was found that was similar to that of the Ugandan president, but it was light-colored, whereas Idi Amin had a penchant for dark cars. Yoni and his men got hold of the car, and on the last day before the operation they managed to paint it black and dry it. . . . Inside the Mercedes there would be an Israeli soldier posing as Idi Amin. This was meant to increase the element of surprise and confusion among the Ugandans and the terrorists.
>
> The idea and its implementation were typical of the unit and of its commander. One of the standing rules was that their skill should not be less than their daring, so they wouldn't have to rely so much on luck.

Maintaining total radio silence as they flew across Africa, the Israeli forces landed at Entebbe an hour before midnight, with their cargo bay doors already open. The black Mercedes with accompanying Land-Rovers rolled down the ramp of the Hercules transport, filled with elite Israeli troops.

The vehicles quickly reached the terminal but two Ugandan sentries, who were aware that Idi Amin had recently purchased a white Mercedes to replace his black one, ordered the motorcade to stop. The sentries were immediately shot dead by the Israeli commandos.

The hostages were in the main hall of the airport building, directly adjacent to the runway. The Israelis sprang from their vehicles and burst into the terminal yelling in Hebrew and English: "Get down! Get down!" A nineteen-year-old French Jew named Jean-

Jacques Maimoni (who chose to identify himself as an Israeli even though he had a French passport), stood up, and was killed by one of the Israeli commandos, who mistook him for a hijacker. Two other hostages, Pasko Cohen, the fifty-two-year-old manager of an Israeli medical insurance fund, and fifty-six-year-old Ida Borochovitch, a Russian Jew who had emigrated to Israel, were killed in the crossfire between the hijackers and the Israeli commandos. At one point, an Israeli commando called out in Hebrew, "Where are the rest of them?" referring to the hijackers. The hostages pointed to the airport's main hall, into which the Israeli commandos threw several hand grenades. They then entered the room and shot the three remaining hijackers, thus completing their assault.

The Israeli assault team sped back to their aircraft and began loading the hostages on board three of the C-130 Hercules transport jets while Ugandan soldiers traded a constant hail of gunfire with them. The Israeli commandos finished the loading and then departed Entebbe Airport. The entire assault lasted less than 30 minutes and all six of the hijackers were killed.

Yonatan Netanyahu was the only Israeli commando who died during the operation. He was killed near the airport entrance, apparently by a Ugandan sniper who fired from the nearby control tower. Five other Israeli commandos were wounded. Out of the 103 hostages, 3 were killed and 10 were wounded. A total of 45 Ugandan soldiers were killed, and 11 Ugandan Army Air Force MiG-17 fighter planes were destroyed on the runways by Israeli commandos while the rescue was in progress. The hundred rescued hostages were flown to Israel via Nairobi.

As we broke the Entebbe raid down into its components, I saw this was no outlandish Hollywood rescue operation, but real-world counterterrorism work at its peak, the simultaneous application of intelligence, obsessive attention to detail, and more than a little luck. One reason the raid was so well planned was that the building in which the hostages were being held was built by an Israeli construction firm. Israeli firms built numerous projects in Africa during the 1960s and 1970s. In this case, the firm still had the blueprints for the terminal, and supplied them to the Israeli cabinet. But, more important, Mossad developed an accurate picture of the whereabouts of the hostages, the number of terrorists, and the involvement of Ugandan troops by immediately interviewing the released hostages in Paris. Luckily, a Jewish Frenchman who'd been mistakenly released with the Christian hostages had military training and a photographic memory, allowing him to give astonishingly precise information about the details on the ground in Uganda. Then the Israeli army built a partial replica of the airport terminal with the help of several engineers who had worked on the actual building.

"Operation Entebbe, with Yoni at its heart, was the first sign to the world at large that one must not give in to terror, that it is possible to overcome it," former prime minister Shimon Peres would later write. "Until then, many had tried to appease terrorists, to give in to their blackmail, to politically capitulate instead of facing them with military might. Operation Entebbe turned out to be a persuasive force for millions of people, proving that the confrontation with trigger-happy terrorists is not a lost battle. In any case, it was a turning point that caused the world to relate differently to the scourge of terrorism and to the criminal mind of its perpetrators. . . . Even the Palestinians, who believed that terror is a result of their tragedy, are now understanding that their tragedy is a result of their reliance on terrorism."

FOURTEEN

From the two platoons of roughly forty guys in basic training, we were down to fourteen real survivors after about two weeks at C.T. School. So the core group who would later form my operational team were all there. We knew we were getting near the finish line, but we were keeping our distance psychologically, knowing that our best buddy could be gone from the base, suddenly, without any good-bye or explanation.

The Krav Maga during basic and advanced training was bad enough, but during Thursday-night sessions at the C.T. School the instructors turned up the dial in terms of aggressiveness and intensity. This was without a doubt the pinnacle of brutality during our entire Special Forces training. It became pure survival in the gym—fight as fiercely as you could or be pummeled into a bruised, bloody, broken heap. The instructors made us go one-on-one against our closest friends—there was no sparring here; nothing sporting about it. We had to kick the shit out of our buddies, fight with genuine ferocity, like one of them just laid his hands on your sister.

Sure, surviving something like this makes for a special bond between you and your teammates, but with every shuddering kick to your rib cage, every attempt to inflict maximum damage, you truly start to hate these guys, at least for the duration of the training. They are genuinely trying to *hurt* you. And many times, they do. In fact, injury is the biggest pitfall from this point on in the training. We actually lost two or three guys from the fractured shins, ribs, and fingers from Thursday-night Krav Maga sessions.

After the Krav instructional, the instructors would send one guy into the center of the ring. Then another one of us would be chosen to go full contact one-on-one until one of us got knocked out. Punching and kicking to the head were not allowed. It's surprisingly hard to knock a guy out with a body shot—you have to connect to his chest, really knock all the wind out of him, in order to score a TKO.

I'd be gasping and limping by this point, but the Krav Maga kept going full-bore. The fight became two-on-one; then three-on-one. The battle culminated with one guy in the middle of the ring, trying to fend off the punches, elbows, and kicks from six of his teammates.

"Fight him! No pitty-pat shit! The whole team—fight!"

Twelve fists, twelve feet, twelve elbows, twelve knees, nothing but a blur of pummeling, elbows swinging, knees flying. It was like a modern-day version of a Roman gladiator school, a freestyle mix of boxing, wrestling, ju-jitsu, karate, and Krav Maga. No pauses; no tap-outs; no punches pulled. Besides intentional head shots, only eye-gouging, hair-pulling, and blows to the balls were off-limits. The instructors goaded us on with rewards: the last man standing—usually crawling—would win a weekend pass. I was bigger than a lot of the other guys, but right away the instructors singled me out as the potential weak link, figured I was some pampered Southern California kid who'd cave when the abuse intensified. Sarcastic Hebrew taunts accompanied the roundhouse punches and sidekicks.

"Think you're tough, Beverly Hills? Jason-fuckin'-Priestley—90210!"

"Aaron! *Ya-kli!*"

"Fuck you, assholes!" I'd shout back, ducking one punch and trying to land a haymaker of my own.

"Brandon!"

"Dylan!"

But I took their best shots, and as those Krav sessions went on, I even began to wear the 90210 nickname with pride.

At the end of the session I'd be in crippling pain, but mentally stronger—telling myself, *I can do this. I can take six guys.* Nothing they can throw at me in the territories can possibly be tougher than what I just did.

In the team-training phase, or *tzevet,* we started doing daily paintball drills—using the mock Arab village at the entrance to the base for the training terrain. This isn't like weekend recreational paintball; the paintball pistols are cranked up to 300 PSI and the balls actually break skin when they hit. We engaged in an all-out war game, pitting five- to eight-man teams against one another. The exercise taught us how to use the advanced shooting skills we practiced individually in a simulation of real-world combat. We learned to surround a house, gain entry through upper-story windows, move methodically through a house, and read all the angles inside a structure so that we would always be covering our team members' backs.

At any time during the C.T. training, the instructors can tap you to draw your weapon, and drop down into a shooting stance. Five instructors then start kicking and punching you mercilessly. You're not shooting live bullets—it's called "shooting dry"—and the goal is to stay in position while under direct assault from multiple sources.

During the six weeks of C.T. School, your bruises never have time to heal. This is the only course in the entire IDF system in which the instructors are allowed—actually encouraged—to hit the trainees. By absorbing the punishment, by not being allowed to hit back, they are converting knee-jerk defense mechanisms into an active, analytical mind-set that allows you to complete the mission despite incredible levels of stress and violent distraction. They're also making you borderline insane.

Our next-to-last assignment was learning to fire accurately from the windows of moving vehicles. We were also learning the hyper-aggressive skills of getaway driving, most of which is deeply counterintuitive, like ramming into a stationary vehicle at maximum velocity, aiming for its rear axle, in order to clear it from a blocked intersection.

The final testing phase at the C.T. School is called the PRAT, a series of very technical qualifications in shooting and gunmanship. One test is a four-minute M-16 drill in which you have to hit several dozen targets. As any veteran cop or soldier can testify, handguns don't always function as they're supposed to. Our C.T. instructors would take ten or twelve guns and create different malfunctions and jams—dirt, sandy grit, a backward-turned bullet. The test required you to grab each gun in turn, identify and fix the malfunction, then fire accurately at the target.

PRAT was two days long, beginning with a team test, incorporating an actual terrorist takedown, a vehicle takedown, and shooting every weapon in our Duvdevan arsenal. Next came the individual test, which is by far the hardest of all the C.T. qualifications.

We were issued a counterterrorist vest, a $1,200 piece of body armor custom-cut for our weapons. All twelve shooting ranges on the base were shut down and each trainee completed the circuit alone, starting at the top of a hill, running a mile down to the base, where the instructors handed him a weapon. You ran to the range, fired at all the targets, sprinted to the next range, received a new weapon, and so on for all twelve ranges. When you'd completed all twelve, you sprinted back up the hill for two minutes of full-contact Krav Maga battle with the instructors.

The whole test lasted only fifteen minutes, but half the guys ended up on their knees at the top of that hill, doubled over, winded, coughing, puking their guts out.

When we'd made it through this final ordeal, the instructors came around to shake our hands. But still there were no certificates, no hats-in-the-air ceremony. Just a terse, "Good job," and then a week off before reporting back to Gibor for the final hurdle, *lochem gimmel*—or third-phase warrior training for the unit.

It was such a relief to know that I'd *made* it to *lochem gimmel*, I almost didn't care what might happen next. All I knew was that the incessant beat-downs and humiliation of our training were over. We were professionals now.

FIFTEEN

From this point forward, almost a year into our army tour, our instructors would concentrate on dialing us in tactically, polishing and refining our C.T. skills, beginning our *real* undercover training. We would begin the transition into full *mista'aravim* mode, a phase lasting six months. We would learn to become expert "Arabists," a skill not possessed by even such elite units as Matkal, Shaldag, and S-13. We would master the art of looking, talking, and acting like Palestinians during undercover operations.

Our first day in the classroom, we were given a strange assignment: go out and rummage through closets and storage bins, trying to round up any out-of-date clothes in our homes or our friends' homes.

"Bring in the oldest shit you can find," the instructor said. "If you can find something from the eighties, all the better. A George

Michael T-shirt, a Duran Duran T-shirt. Shit that might not even fit properly, anything you can pull together."

When we came back to the base with all our piles of clothes, the instructor started the sorting process. Eighty percent of the stuff ended up on the floor. He was very selective. "No, no, they'd never wear this"—zeroing in on a certain look: Timberland shirts, really outdated Jordache and Guess jeans, the stuff you tend to find in the impoverished towns of the territories that looks, smells, and feels authentic.

The next day they brought in an Arab vehicle—not a prop car, but an old, beat-up 1982 Mercedes that the Israelis impounded from some Palestinians at a checkpoint. Onions and garlic were hanging inside, Arabic newspapers were on the floor; the whole car had a nasty overheated perspiration-soaked odor.

Sticking his head inside, Shimon, one of the cockiest of the trainees, made a scowling face."Shit, this car *stinks*."

The instructor teed off on him.

"Oh, you think so? Should we have the car *cleaned* for you? Want me to go get the wet-dry vacuum?" Shimon stood there speechless, blinking at the instructor. "That's the way it's *supposed* to smell, you fucking idiot!"

Back in the classroom, things quickly got serious as we learned about the nuances of Palestinian life: their culture, customs, and beliefs. The instructors explained which covers were most advantageous to working in the territories: The seventy-year-old man sipping his strong black coffee at a sidewalk table; the university-age religious student coming out of the mosque; the mentally retarded teenager—there's a high degree of mental retardation in certain Palestinian communities—all disguises that wouldn't attract too much attention from passersby. More important, we could have the best undercover disguise and makeup in the world, but if we fundamentally misplayed our roles—did something that would be completely out of character—we would not only blow our cover but run the risk of jeopardizing a lot of lives.

For example, we would often take on the role of an older, religious Palestinian man, wearing a keffiyeh, because in the Palestinian culture old men are granted the highest degree of respect. Sometimes, another Duvdevan operator would take on the role of the wife. Since Palestinian life, like many cultures in the Arab-speaking world, is totally male-dominated, we had to remember that the man would *always* walk a few steps in front of the woman. This tiny detail was rehearsed over and over, and we often worked in pairs during undercover missions, posing as an old married couple. It would have been a dead giveaway to any Palestinians in the street if the "female" Duvdevan operator had the audacity to keep in step with her "husband," rather than following the requisite few feet to the rear.

To pull off a female disguise, the instructors naturally chose shorter men—five-five, five-six—with the slightest frames. To pull off an old man's disguise, they looked for guys with prematurely weathered faces. A lot of the kibbutz kids were selected for that role since they had crow's-feet from spending so much time in the unrelenting Middle Eastern sun.

We spent long days in class learning how to apply makeup correctly, relying heavily on Tan No. 4, an olive-colored foundation that the fairer, Ashkenazi kids, like me, put on their neck, forearms, and hands. There was a gorgeous twenty-year-old female soldier in charge of handling the makeup duties for our entire unit. She'd been sent to an advanced course to learn to mix and blend Hollywood-quality stage makeup. Before an operation, she was responsible for perfectly transforming ten or twelve guys, at least until some of us became proficient in doing our own makeup. She showed us how to use mustard glue to attach false beards and mustaches, how to black out one of our teeth so that, for a crucial split second, we'd look like some poor Palestinian kid with bad dental hygiene. There were different nuances and specifics to learn for each town and region: In Jenin you'll see a lot of beards with no mustaches, just a clean-shaven upper-lip, a very old-school Palestinian look. You won't see that as often in a more modern city like Hebron, and you'll almost never see it in Ramallah, which is a supermodern city, almost like Tel Aviv.

Similarly, there are different types of dress in various parts of the territories. The red-and-white keffiyehs are dominant in some parts, black-and-white or green-and-white in still others. Red-and-white means the neighborhood supports Hamas; black-and-white means it supports Fatah; green-and-white, which can be seen much less frequently, means Hezbollah. We would know in advance which areas we'd be going into on a mission, and if the color of our keffiyehs wasn't correct, we'd have gotten fucked up quick.

During scenario training, we watched hours upon hours of surveillance footage, studying the operations of previous undercover teams, breaking down snatch-and-grabs that went well and ones that didn't. We analyzed every body movement and facial expression, the distinctive way an older man at a sidewalk café flipped open his newspaper and held his demitasse of black coffee, or the stoop-shouldered, world-weary gait of a woman in her mid-fifties.

In one class, the instructors brought in two Druze from the border patrol, and they showed us some of the secret techniques they used to infiltrate Palestinian crowds, the details of which, unfortunately, are too classified to print here.

Culturally speaking, the Arabs are proud and close-knit, the neighborhoods tend to be tiny, and everyone knows everyone's business. In the territories, you may have four or five interrelated families living in the same apartment building. Therefore undercover operators, no matter how convincingly disguised, will still be spotted very quickly as outsiders, meaning they don't have a second to waste.

One of the hotbeds of recruitment to radical Islamist movements are the universities, and we watched a lot of video footage of Palestinian students. The students are among the most aggressive members of their society; they have a strongly articulated sense of self, hair-trigger reaction times, and are very prone to fight back in an altercation.

"Anytime you're attempting an operation at a university," the instructor told us, "expect to get mobbed. These kids will be swarming you in seconds."

We studied the Koran, memorizing a few important passages, learning how the religion informs daily behavior in the Occupied Territories. Again, the instructors had pragmatic goals; they were not trying to turn us overnight into experts in Islamic theology. We focused on what Islam's sacred texts say about the Jews—and what this Muslim worldview means out there in the field.

To my mind, one of the most surprising things we learned was that the Palestinians weren't intimidated by us. They wouldn't flee or cower, or even necessarily answer questions, just because they were confronted with an IDF uniform.

"They're not afraid of you," our instructors said over and over. "They're not scared because you're Israeli. More important, they're not afraid of the IDF."

Why this lack of fear given the overwhelming might of the Israeli army, its record of military victories over the past sixty years, and the unapologetic stance taken by every soldier in the face of Palestinian hostility? Primarily it comes from the Arabs historic sense of pride in relation to the Jewish people. It's an immense disgrace for the Palestinians to be ruled by Jews. The instructors drilled it into our heads that long before there was a State of Israel, long before the British Empire took control of the Holy Land after World War I, there were unbroken centuries of Muslim rule—from the golden era of Saladin defeating the Crusaders through the Ottoman Empire's rule into the early twentieth century. During this period, Jews were a tiny minority within the greater Arab culture, protected and even respected to varying degrees as "People of the Book," but nonetheless regarded as second-class citizens. Jews were seen as a people without any tradition of military conquest for nearly two millennia. Then came the tremendous shock of the Jewish military victories in the War of Independence in 1948 and the Six-Day War in 1967, when the Palestinian cities, towns, and villages of the West Bank and Gaza were suddenly overrun by Israeli tanks and infantry. Therein lies the sense of humiliation the Palestinians feel on a daily basis. Not a moment goes by when that sense of humiliation is not uppermost in their collective consciousness. Especially for young males, being detained and interviewed for hours at a time, being under the physical control of Jews, is tantamount to being a slave. Their pride, autonomy, even their sense of manhood have been stripped from them. So they are fearless, often reckless, when confronted by Israeli soldiers, picking up rocks, bricks, bottles, anything they can turn into a homemade weapon to use against our state-of-the-art military machine.

After we completed the cultural primer, our linguistic courses began in earnest. We started with basic conversational Arabic. We were taught phonetic Arabic, no reading and writing, since literacy plays little part in undercover work. It's much more important to comprehend and immerse yourself in the conversations around you on the street.

Although these Arabic lessons, taught by the top Arabists in the IDF rather than members from Duvdevan, involved no advanced technology or cutting-edge weaponry, they were the most technical aspect of our training. As any visitor to Israel quickly learns, there's a fair amount of Arabic incorporated into modern Hebrew—especially curse words, drug and nightclub slang—but *mista'aravim* work requires much more than this basic level. We have to be able to talk comfortably and conversationally during an operation, say: "Hey, what's up? Good to see you. Didn't we meet a few months back at the mosque?" In addition, we have to pay close attention to the nuances of speech, the types of phrases appropriate to an older man, a middle-aged woman, or a university student. Our interactions with strangers might only last a second or two, but in that brief moment, we convey an entire life story through verbal cues and body language. If the slightest detail is off, you'll raise a red flag.

Think of the wide disparity in regional accents in the United States alone, let alone the distinct speech patterns and slang of an Australian, Canadian, or Scotsman. The same is true of Arabic: there are numerous dialects, regional distinctions, and accents. To play the role of a Palestinian who was born and raised in the West Bank, the accent has to be *perfect*. If you can't master that accent, you won't be deployed in that aspect of an undercover team. It's just not worth the risk.

Our instructors rigorously focused on each man's individual strengths, picking out guys with the most natural talent for any given component of an undercover mission. Ironically, the Sephardic trainees whose parents or grandparents had been born in Arabic-speaking countries like Morocco, Egypt, or Syria often spoke excellent Arabic, but their accent was completely wrong—it wasn't anything like a Palestinian accent. They seemingly had an advantage, but in reality they were dead in the water. The instructors would rather start with a blank slate, taking a guy with zero Arabic and teaching him from scratch to sound like a Palestinian. Trying to unlearn an accent you've had since childhood is nearly impossible.

Book smarts don't really matter in the linguistic course; the real determining factor is whether you have a musical ear for languages. It's an innate talent. I have some musical ability and, after a lot of repetition, I could nail the Arabic with near perfection. The hardest part for me was that everything was written out in phonetic Hebrew, and the level at which I could read and write Hebrew was still far below everyone else's in my training unit. But with the spoken Arabic lessons, I was in the top 20 percent of the class. The very best were the Ashkenazi Sabras who'd studied Arabic as a second language in high school just as we'd study Spanish or French in the United

States—taught by Israeli teachers who'd learned to speak with a pure Palestinian accent.

In their tireless search for *individual* strengths, the Israeli Special Forces are diametrically opposed to the U.S. Navy SEALs and British SAS models, with their famous emphasis on instilling multidimensional, broad-based skills in all Special Force operators. In Israel, they don't try to mold everybody into all-purpose supercommandos or Hebrew-speaking versions of James Bond. Almost from the outset at C.T. School, the instructors started making talent-driven decisions to determine who should fulfill which missions. Certain guys were physically suited to playing a woman or an old man; others delivered the Palestinian dialect so convincingly they could engage in more interactive undercover roles without ever tipping their hand; guys with superior marksmanship or driving skills worked the perimeter without donning a fake beard or opening their mouths to speak Arabic.

For example, Ehud Barak, the most decorated soldier in the country's history, was a regular infantryman before he was recruited into Sayeret Matkal. Before that, he'd been a locksmith on his kibbutz, and could pick locks as well as any cat burglar. It was said the Arabs couldn't make a lock that Barak couldn't get through, an incredibly valuable skill in a tiny country with finite resources, where locksmithing had rarely been practiced by European immigrant Jews, who tended to be trained in more traditional jobs in the garment industry, or as jewelers, bookkeepers, and schoolteachers. The Special Forces philosophy became: Cultivate individual strengths, look for natural talent. Don't waste time and resources forcing a square peg into a round hole.

Naturally, there were a lot of recruits who simply couldn't pull off a *Mista'aravim* disguise. We'd stand there laughing at them, practically pissing ourselves, because they looked so ludicrous in flowing robes, sprouting fake facial hair, and speaking Arabic like a bad Berlitz tape. But then other kids could walk out and your jaw would drop at the transformation.

Take Dedi Ben Hannania. Dedi was one of the best on the team at playing the part of a woman. Dedi was a swarthy, fine-featured Kurdish-Iraqi Jew who gave up a career as a professional soccer player—he'd been offered a contract with one of the top professional clubs in Israel—to serve in the IDF. Standing five eleven, rail thin but well muscled, Dedi was easily the most gifted athlete in the unit. He was also the biggest practical joker and wise ass on the team, a time-honored characteristic in Israeli culture known as pulling *zubut*.

Dedi would walk out dressed as a woman, hunching down under his flowing dress and limping along on a cane like an old grandmother on her way to market in Jenin.

"Salaam aleikum," Dedi would say, in a pitch-perfect Palestinian half-whisper, eyes downcast humbly, struggling with his groceries.

Then, he'd shift gears suddenly from being an old woman, his cane clattering to the linoleum, and morph into a belly-dancing, eyelash-batting tease, shimmying and throwing his hips around the classroom. As a gifted athlete, Dedi was also an amazing dancer. We'd playfully throw kisses his way. "Come here, sweetheart," Ilan would say, but I jumped up and made my move first, pawing at Dedi's stuffed bra and padded hips.

Life-or-death operation or not, there's no denying this: the whole process *is* funny—you're putting on fake boobs and wiggling your ass into pantyhose; the very act of dressing up as a woman makes you feel like a complete idiot.

Over time, my commanders began to realize that my own strengths lay less in the undercover mode than in the takedown teams, the explosive, lightning-quick, fully geared-up tactical stage of the operation. It's arguably the most dangerous part of the job, being the first, second, or third man through the blown door, leveling the short M-16 and screaming in Arabic: "*Jesh! Jesh!* We're the army! Where are you hiding Mahmoud?"

Yet for all the time we spend perfecting our Palestinian dialect, it's always preferable to do no talking whatsoever during a mission. Simplicity is always the best—and safest—policy. Our commanders would often take some of the Sephardic guys who physically look most like Arabs—and a lot of people in Israel joke that the Sephardim actually *are* ethnically Arabs—dress them up as university students and send them onto the street to act as the eyes-on-target. They never opened their mouths, never interacted with a single Arab. During my time as a fully operational warrior in the unit, I came to see that the missions where the talking and playacting were kept to a bare minimum tended to go the smoothest.

Next, we were ordered to stop shaving and we were issued our special passes to exempt us from the typical clean-shaven IDF requirement. I didn't use a razor for another five months. Guys who could grow the heaviest beards, usually the Sephardim, had a much better chance of passing as a religious Arab man. Some of the Ashkenazi guys had such wispy, fair-colored beards that they were soon ordered to shave again, and those with a slight build usually specialized in passing for Palestinian women.

Day by day, the instructors unlocked more nuances about the

Palestinian culture, tiny things you'd never notice unless you're trained, like the fact that many young Palestinian men play soccer, giving them a distinct strut from bouncing lightly on the balls of their feet. While the best disguise for a Duvdevan man posing as a Palestinian consists of nothing more complicated than blue jeans, a white T-shirt, and a super-cheesy black leather jacket, we learned to always buy the correct brand of shoes. The economy is so bad in the territories that almost no one can afford top-shelf brands like Nike, Adidas, or Puma. They wear cheap Chinese-made knockoffs. Those no-name sneakers are a dead giveaway. Time and again, the Border Patrol will catch a suicide bomber on the way from the territories to detonate himself in Tel Aviv disguised as an IDF soldier but still wearing those cheap knockoff sneakers on his feet.

By the time we were only a couple weeks away from graduation, we started to sense a new attitude among the warriors who'd been our instructors: there was practically no psychological distance. They'd begun to treat us as human beings. There was a degree of respect between teacher and student. We were not at their level—not even close—but they appreciated the fact that we'd survived fourteen months of grueling training, and better than anyone, they knew what an accomplishment that was. On the other hand, there was a whole *other* degree of respect that they didn't give us, one we wouldn't earn until we'd started working in the field.

When we were on the firing range, they were no longer smacking our heads and kicking us in the ribs. They were treating us like professionals, imparting little gems they'd accrued over years of performing missions.

"Okay, guys, today don't forget the importance of proper finger control. A straight shot doesn't come from squeezing the trigger, but from gently pushing it backward toward you, while remembering your breathing. . . ."

We spent a half hour focusing on the few millimeters of movement in our trigger fingers. By the end of the day, I could shoot with my eyes closed and surround the bull's eye with a tight cluster of holes.

And yet we still were not allowed to look the veteran fighters directly in the face, an irritating little piece of hierarchical ball-busting that some guys never seemed to master, even though the rule went into effect on day one of basic training. If you accidentally made eye contact, you had to drop to your knees, put your hands straight in the air, and wait as the other guy either punched you in the stomach or smacked you in the back of the head. This was more like fraternity hazing than the sadistic beatings we endured at the C.T. School, but it certainly kept us humble.

For our first formal undercover job, the instructors sent us into East Jerusalem, which is an Israeli-controlled but nearly 100 percent Arab environment. The Israeli army has a constant visible presence in that quarter of the Old City, but it's still an extremely dangerous section for Jews to travel through. Most Israelis, even lifelong residents of Jerusalem, have never set foot in East Jerusalem—and for good reason. Many of the ancient stone walls along those cramped, narrow streets bear Magen David markers, small plaques memorializing murdered Jews.

This time around, of course, we were not in the controlled environment of the classroom. We were dressed in our eighties hand-me-down clothes, the acid-washed Guess jeans with frayed hems, the cheap knockoff sneakers. There was still no mission objective beyond hanging out, loitering around some sesame cart on the corner, throwing out a few basic lines in a Palestinian dialect.

"Salaam aleikum, akhooee? Keef halak? Inta mabsoot?"

Nothing fancier than: "What's up? How are you doing? You happy?"

If the people we were talking to came back with too many suspicious questions, we were ordered to abort and walk directly back to our rendezvous point.

We were not armed while in disguise, but a few instructors, dressed as Arabs and carrying concealed pistols, were watching us from a safe perimeter. It was like a classroom in the field: the instructors were still evaluating us, grading us, trying to see who had the natural inclination to work undercover and who would be better suited for the takedown or sniping teams.

The first few times you encounter an actual group of Palestinians, you don't open your mouth because you're fucking scared. You gradually build up your courage; you buy some sweet corn, stroll to a stand for an Arabic newspaper, tell an old religious man you hope he's enjoying this perfect weather.

By the second or third time we were undercover in East Jerusalem, I was approached by a young guy about my age, and I said, "Hey, what's up?" in Arabic.

He replied in such a torrent of rapid-fire Arabic that I had to make a snap decision to improvise, switch languages midgame.

"D'you speak English, man?" I said. "I'm Palestinian, but I'm from the States."

"Where in the States?" He spoke fair English himself, albeit with a heavy accent.

"I live in California, but I'm here for a few weeks, visiting my grandfather in Ramallah."

He locked his jet black eyes on me, then nodded, told me to enjoy my time in Palestine.

It was such a relief to see that my story, look, and attitude seemed to pass muster. I hadn't drawn too much attention to myself, I hadn't panicked when questioned, and I was able to make it back to the rendezvous point around the corner with my skin intact.

We were still a few weeks away from graduation when we received our special permits to carry handguns and started dressing in what's called "Maday Bet"—Uniform B. This was the standard uniform we would wear during field operations: green fatigues, black New Balance sneakers, and a customized leather gun belt worn only by Special Forces soldiers with an inside-the-waistband holster and a custom-cut holder for the extra clip that goes on the small of your back, just toward your gun side.

The veteran Duvdevan operators took us each aside and showed us how to adjust our uniform. They explained that the red combat boots would only be worn on special occasions, that we should tuck our coveted red beret under our left epaulette and wear our guns concealed on the right-hand side. I remember Ilan grabbing me roughly by the shoulders just outside the barracks, tugging at my green T-shirt, and tucking it in over the gun butt, so that nothing was visible besides a faint square bulge at the hip.

"Good, Aaron," Ilan said, smiling as he gave me a final once-over. "Now you don't look like John Wayne. You actually look like a warrior."

Just as the finish line was in sight, we were ordered on one final forced march. Even though it was just five kilometers, this was one of the hardest marches I ever did—next to the *massa kumta*, of course—because each of us had to carry a sixty-pound jerry can full of water. Plus, your body is loaded down with your gear and guns, weighing another seventy pounds.

We finished around two A.M., collapsed on our asses, chests heaving, tilting our canteens of lukewarm water to our lips. We were too exhausted to fully understand what a milestone we'd reached.

I was physically spent, half-nodding off in the dirt, when the cacophony of screaming and car horns jolted me upright. Then, out of nowhere, all the seasoned warriors showed up in their souped-up SUVs and the beat-up Peugeots, fully undercover, dressed as Arabs. In my half-delirium, I almost thought we were being swarmed by a band of terrorists who'd breached the base's security perimeter. Their heads were wrapped in keffiyehs, rifles and short M-16s in their hands. They were driving around us in circles, kicking up clouds of dirt and grit until it was impossible to see three feet in front of your face.

In the midst of this surreal scene, a delicious smell reached me, and I saw that there was a feast waiting for us: steak, falafel, hummus, pita, trays of cookies, cakes, and assorted fruit. Then the general who was the head of the Central Command showed up in his tinted-window Mercedes, smoking a cigarette. He opened the door and got out, followed by a bunch of colonels.

And then they lit up a thirty-foot-high Duvdevan insignia crafted from wire, a towering metal sculpture lined with diesel-soaked cloth. I will never forget the disgusting diesel smoke, choking our lungs at two A.M., the moment they set that thing ablaze. The flames leapt higher and higher against that surreal nighttime landscape, and my heart began to race with the realization that I'd finally made it, that in a few hours I would officially be inducted as a member of Duvdevan.

The next morning Ilan and a few of the other lieutenants and sergeants came around officially issuing our short M-16s and our handguns. The unit insignias had been pinned on our uniforms, covered with a strip of white cloth tape.

We gathered in formation up on the hill. The general gave a brief speech, then they raised the Duvdevan flag alongside the Israeli flag. We burst into song, the national anthem, "Hatikvah." And at the end of the two-hour ceremony we all simultaneously peeled the cloth tape from our uniforms to reveal the unit insignia.

The general's announcement was succinct: "That's it—you've officially graduated."

The moment they announced that we had graduated, that we were officially now operational members of the unit, we all threw our red berets in the air, then formed a tight circle, hugging each other, tears streaming down our faces. It was an amazing, indescribable feeling—a private moment between the trainees.

No one spoke for a long time, knowing that we were now bonded together for life.

Behind us, we could hear all the veteran warriors getting in their vehicles, revving their engines, and taking off. They didn't stop to wish us good luck, shake our hands, or even offer a good-bye. It actually made me smile: I realized that they didn't give a fuck about our little sentimental group hug, our tear-streaked and sunburned faces, our intense rite of passage. For them, this was just another morning: time to get back to work, time to plan and execute more counterterrorism missions. I realized that we weren't anything special to them; we weren't their band of brothers. They'd had their own ceremonies, their own time to bond, their own communal moments.

This one was just about us.

SIXTEEN

After graduation we were given ten days off to recharge our batteries, after which we were responsible for getting our asses back to base on time—no more military buses.

"Be back on the base the Sunday after next," Ilan said. "Meet at the flagpole. You're going to get your new room assignment and find out who you're bunking with."

Since we would be passing though the territories every time we returned to the base, and since we would never wear anything identifying us as Israeli military, Ilan started to question us about taking adequate security precautions whenever we returned from a leave. He went around the barracks in turn, asking us all how we would be getting back to the base the following Sunday.

Some guys had their own cars, some were getting lifts, some were taking taxis.

"What about you, Aaron?" Ilan asked.

"I'm going to ride my bike."

Ilan stared hard. Those pale blue eyes never failed to give me a chill.

"What kind of bike?"

"RF600."

"You brought it from L.A.?"

"Yeah." At that time, I don't think there was another brand-new RF600 in all of Israel. "Listen," I said. "Anytime you want to, you can take it out."

"Give me your gun," Ilan said.

I drew my Sig Sauer from the holster. Ilan took it from my hand, popped out the clip, and made certain that the magazine was topped off.

"When you're riding through the territories, always make sure your ammo is topped off," he said. "Listen to me—what are you smiling at? Do I look like I'm fucking joking? When you come to a stop sign or a red light, don't stop. *Ever.* You run through them. If a Palestinian cop chases you, don't pull over either. Just get back to the base and we'll sort it out with the cops."

I decided to spend my two Shabbats on leave with Golda. Since my months on the kibbutz, I'd been keeping in fairly close contact with her; I would often stop by her sprawling, luxurious apartment in Givatayim on my three-day leaves. Golda treated me like I'd never had an older woman treat me. It wasn't quite a mother-son relationship or that of grandmother and grandson. She was more like one of your friend's mothers who constantly overbabies you whenever you set foot in her place. *Aaron, sit down! What do you want to eat? What do you want to drink? You look so tired—should I make Turkish coffee?*

I sensed that she felt guilty about her own son who was about ten years older than me—she'd been working too hard, traveling too much as a Mossad operative, to be a dedicated mother.

As soon as I pushed open her apartment door, the mouthwatering smells would hit me: she'd been in the kitchen for hours, preparing roast chicken, hummus, tahini; there'd be fresh pitas warming in the oven, a pot of rice or herb-flavored couscous rattling on the stove. Then she'd sit me down in her dining room and serve me one of those overflowing, home-cooked Israeli meals—the kind you crave like nothing else when you've been living on army rations, the kind where you have to push your chair away from the table with a groan, loosen your belt, and find you can't move your legs for several hours afterward.

I knew that Golda had seen a lot of action in her Mossad service, before a terrorist attack in North Africa left her hobbling on her prosthetic hip. She was a by-the-book Mossad operative, never talking about what she'd been involved in, but I gleaned that she'd taken part in some of the most dramatic counterterrorism operations of the 1970s. She was stationed in Africa for a long time, but she'd also been in South America, hunting down Josef Mengele and other Nazi war criminals hiding out in Argentina and Paraguay.

By the time we became tight, she wasn't a *katsa*—a field operative—any longer, and I could tell she missed the action, that she liked being around young, neat, strong, well-put-together soldiers. I could tell it made her feel youthful again.

I never needed a formal invitation to drop by, but sometimes I'd call ahead and tell her to expect company. "Listen," I would say. "I'm coming with one friend, but you might want to cook some extra just in case."

She would laugh, knowing my game full well. "Yes, Aaron, I'll cook some extra."

Then I'd show up with half my team, five or six guys—Dedi, Inon, Nir, Shechman, Yossi. But Golda loved it! Her whole apartment would suddenly be filled with nineteen- and twenty-year-old commandos, slinging their short M-16s in the corner, smoking, singing, piling up huge plates of roast chicken and couscous in the kitchen. Someone would be switching CDs in the stereo, and if Ilan came with us, he'd grab one of us at random and start dancing. Cigarette dangling from his lip, Ilan would waltz cheek-to-cheek, with me or Dedi or Yossi, from the living room out onto the open balcony.

Golda would be sitting back in an armchair, watching all of us with a big smile. She was a very quiet, introspective woman but she loved nothing more than to entertain a bunch of young soldiers like that. Even though I was benefiting from her generosity, I also felt like I was somehow repaying her for all she'd done for me.

Since I'd leapt headlong into military training, I'd missed out on a lot of the routine, day-to-day cultural aspects of being a well-rounded Israeli. Golda took it upon herself to give me a Sabra's education. For example, I never had any taste for Israeli music, whereas most Israelis tend to get extremely passionate—choking up, tears welling, swept away with the emotion of the lyrics—when they're listening to their favorite singers, Naomi Shemer, Yehoram Gaon, Esther Ofarim, Chava Alberstein. Golda and I would sit in her living room, on her beautiful Scandinavian furniture, with a stunning view of the Mediterranean Sea behind us, and she would play me her entire record collection. I loved one in particular, "Day Dreamer," by Yehuda Poliker—a folk singer of Greek-Jewish ancestry—that she used to play over and over. We'd stand out on the balcony, smoking, talking, listening to Yehuda Poliker strumming the bouzouki and singing "After the War."

Sometimes, I would sing along with the lyrics. My Hebrew had become so much better, so much more natural and confident, that she beamed with pride. "You know something? I speak to you now, Aaron, and I feel like I'm speaking to a real Sabra," she said. "I don't feel like I'm talking to a visitor anymore."

Her Mossad training showed, too, in that she would *never* ask me about the unit. It was an unspoken boundary between us. If there was something I felt like telling her, I'd feel free to confide it; but she knew enough not to ask me about army life. She'd ask mostly about my mother:

"What does your mother think about what you're doing? She must be worried about you, Aaron—are you able to call her often?"

I told her that communicating with my mother was frustrating. I'd call home as often as I could from the base but my mother would ask me general questions about politics in the Middle East—"So what do you think of the peace process?"—when all my daily reality consisted of was learning how to apply makeup and dress like a Palestinian Arab, or getting my ass kicked every Thursday in the Krav Maga session. All our phone calls from the base were being monitored for security reasons, so there was nothing I could tell her about what I was going through on a physical or emotional level. The superficiality of our phone calls, roughly once a month, made me feel even more estranged.

Sometimes, Golda would ask about the friends I'd made on the kibbutz. "Do you keep in touch with the guys back at the fishpond? How are Dror and those Weiss boys doing?"

Golda knew enough about the Special Forces training, and about my unit in particular, to understand that deep undercover work takes a serious emotional toll, even if you had family and a strong support system of friends to fall back on. Without any family in the country, she knew I was dancing along a precipice. She also noticed that the more time I'd spent training with the unit, the more introverted and serious I'd become. There was a darkness hanging over my mood at all times.

One night on her balcony during that ten-day leave, I opened up to Golda, told her how close to the breaking point I had felt right at the end of the training, wondering: *Is it worth eating all this shit?* It was the onset of a kind of post-training depression, a crashing sense of pointlessness. I would look around the barracks at night and feel like such an outsider. Most of the Israeli guys seemed so mentally strong, so self-confident, they didn't seem to be racked by the doubts I was feeling. My body was hardened from the fourteen months of training, but my mind felt like Jell-O.

I decided to confide in Golda something I would never have admitted to anyone in the unit, the lowest moment I'd felt in all the months since the *gibush* at Wingate. It happened two weeks before the graduation ceremony when the instructors ordered us to do one final *socio-meter.*

"There was this one kid named Shimon," I told her. "Solid as a rock in training, a great athlete, perfect marksman, a beast in every physical challenge."

He passed his *gibush* and started his training with Matkal. Then he was dropped. At that point he was given his choice of assignments. "Look, if I'm not going to be Matkal," Shimon had said, "then I'll go to Duvdevan. It's a great unit, very similar work, a lot of action." Shimon was what's called a *tzvon-bon,* meaning a rich Ashkenazi punk from north of Tel Aviv. Basically, it's like being from Beverly Hills, which made Shimon the Israeli version of me, the guy with the silver spoon in his mouth, who's had every door opened for him, always acting *tafas tachat*, which literally translates as "grabbing ass," but simply means somebody who thinks their shit doesn't stink.

"Shimon had a massive chip on his shoulder," I told Golda. "He was so *tafas tachat* all the time, never dropped that Matkal attitude. Two weeks before graduation, when we're asked to put someone's head on the chopping block, it was obvious that a lot of guys were thinking of voting Shimon out of the unit."

When it came time for the secret ballot in that final *socio-meter*, I don't know what came over me, but I didn't want to vote out Shimon. I didn't want to vote out *anyone*. I was beyond caring. As they say in Israel, "my dick was broken"—that's the translation of the Hebrew phrase *zayin nishbar*, literally, "my cock is busted." Every ounce of motivation was gone. I didn't care if they sent me packing the next morning, if they transferred me out to the paratroopers, Nahal, Golani, or a tank platoon.

"I was so tired of the whole process that I couldn't bring myself to vote for Shimon," I told Golda. "So I wrote my own name on the slip of paper, drew a goddamned smiley face next to it, and then dropped it in the hat."

But as expected, everyone else had thrown Shimon's name into the hat. Two weeks from the end, Shimon disappeared from the base. No good-bye, no hugs, no handshake. We never saw him again. Rumors circulated that he wound up going into the *Misrad ha-Bitahon*, Israel's Department of Defense, and ultimately landed as a *jobnik* with Mossad.

As I opened up about my level of post-training depression, Golda nodded, smiling, putting her hand on my forearm. She understood better than anyone that level of psychological exhaustion. She watched with her huge, hooded brown eyes—knowing, empathetic, classically beautiful Jewish eyes. And sometimes just from the way she looked at me, I could tell that she thought I was a lost soul but, despite the psychic toll of training I emerged from those fourteen months knowing I had found the one thing that I was born to do. For the first time in my life, I felt like the opposite of a lost soul.

The ex-fighters up at the kibbutz fishpond had tried to analyze me, too. They thought I was nuts, but it was a kind of craziness and a passion that they respected—*That Cohen, he's fuckin' meshugge!*

Golda tried to get a little deeper, do some psychological digging on me, based, I suppose, on her extensive intel background. It's a natural thing for a Mossad operative to do—run a psychological profile, try to excavate the inner man behind the facade. She believed that for a nice young man to reject a comfortable life in America, to leave his family behind, and to come do something so hard, so dangerous, then something must have been wrong at home.

Golda was right of course. But I wasn't ready to talk to her—to talk to anyone at that point—about the truth. Clearly I was getting something vital out of the Israeli army that I hadn't gotten from my dysfunctional show-business family back in L.A. But the bottom line for me was this: I'd never been happier. I had earned a place among the world's best fighters, and I had been granted tremendous responsibilities to do an important job. I loved being accepted into Duvdevan more than anything I could ever have imagined.

The more I visited Golda during my pre-operational phase with the unit, the more I noticed a profound sadness whenever she looked at me. I'm over thirty today, and I understand now what she was feeling. Back then, as a nineteen-and-a-half-year-old kid, awash in ambition and testosterone, I couldn't understand her concern. But it was nothing more complicated than: *This kid could be dead a year from now.*

She knew what it meant to be a fighter in the IDF. She knew the Israeli mentality and, more important, she knew the Arab mentality. She'd spent forty years fighting the same war I was just about to join and you could see her weariness with it all—the fanaticism, the ancient hatreds, the never-ending bloodshed. In those forty years, she'd seen a lot of good men die.

Only a woman who'd done what she'd done could appreciate the danger I was in. So enjoy this food, her brown eyes seemed to say, enjoy this music, enjoy this cigarette. I might never see you again. It's a quintessentially Israeli attitude: Let's seize the moment *now*; let's live right *now*.

Sadly, as I finished training and started to go out on undercover missions, Golda subtly started the process of disconnecting from me. Over the next few months, we stopped speaking on a regular basis. I stopped coming by for Shabbat during my leaves from the unit. She'd begun to care about me about me like a member of her family, and she couldn't stand the thought of me coming back from the territories in a fucking wooden box.

PART III

SEVENTEEN

On our first day as operators in the unit, Ilan, our first lieutenant, and Boaz, the sergeant-major who'd made the big announcement about me coming from California my first day of basic training, came around issuing special pagers to all the new men.

"Anytime this pager goes off," Ilan said, "you drop everything and call back. No matter where you are—you call back to the base. I don't care if you're just about to get in the sack with the hottest chick you've ever seen, you throw on your fucking clothes and get back to the base within three hours of the page."

Ilan wasn't just busting our balls. The pager means one of two things: there's a hostage situation involving an Israeli civilian or military personnel somewhere in the territories, or the unit is about to be deployed against such a high-profile terrorist target that the command feels it's necessary to bring in several teams on the mission.

Except for emergency situations like those, life in the unit is like any other job: there's an established rhythm and routine to the fieldwork. Each operational team works on a three-week cycle. The first week you're in training, the second week you're in operations, the third week you're on "Ready 5 Status," which means you're not allowed to leave the base in case you're needed on backup. You play volleyball or *shesh-besh*—backgammon—smoke cigarettes, do fuck-all, and wait for that pager to start beeping.

And yet the pace is surprisingly brisk, especially during the countless hours you're required to be shooting guns at the firing range. It's estimated that every Special Forces soldier costs Israel between $500,000 and $1 million (U.S.) to train, feed, and house, so we must continually hone those perishable skills. Think of it as a boxer who's trained six or eight months for a championship prizefight; in the final days, his training regimen might lighten somewhat, but he can't afford to stop hitting the speed bag and doing six miles a day of roadwork.

I was eating lunch in the mess hall my first week as a fully operational warrior when word came down that we were going out on our first mission.

"Tonight—2100! Get all your shit ready," Ilan said.

We had three hours to get our gear together. Everyone was in tactical green, game faces on, ready to roll. We met in the operations room. When I walked in there were already a couple of teams sitting and waiting. Assignments were being handed out: My job was going to be on a support team, going into a Hamas neighborhood in Ramallah. I wouldn't be undercover, or working the entry-and-extraction team. I'd be responsible for securing the perimeter while an entry team pulled a terrorist suspect out of a house.

The senior team members told us what to pack, what not to pack, and stripped our gear down to the bare essentials so that we weren't loaded down with equipment we wouldn't need. Ilan called us into the debriefing room, pulling out an aerial photograph.

"Here's what we're going to do," he said, gesturing to me and the guys on my squad, designated as *Gimmel*, or C Team, for the operation. "We're going to drop you three or four blocks away. Here's the navigation point. Study it well. C Team, you're going to run up the street. Then you're going to wait for B Team. B Team's going to stack up on the door. The moment B Team gets there, if anyone shoots in your direction, C Team, you have orders to engage right away. No hesitation."

We piled into one of our white panel vans and headed to Ramallah. Taking my seat in the van next to Yossi and Inon, I felt my heart pounding wildly. Silence. No small talk between the new team members. There was no denying it, though no one acknowledged it either, but we were all frightened. We were like brand-new actors showing up for the first time on a movie set—nervous, skittish, waiting for the director to tell us what to do.

There were five of us in our van. Three other vans held fifteen more warriors, making this a mission with two complete Duvdevan teams. One undercover team had gone into the neighborhood earlier. They were already in place, disguised as Palestinian civilians, serving as eyes-on-the-target in the half hour before we arrived on the scene. Throughout the drive to Ramallah, they kept radioing back to us the all-clear:

"Nobody's come or gone out. No movement around the house."

I glanced out the window at the scenes speeding past: mounds of burning garbage everywhere, red graffiti scrawled on walls, old men sitting on stools in the shadows of streetlights, playing backgammon, puffing hand-rolled cigarettes, and everywhere I looked, packs of wild, mangy dogs. It was an impoverished, depressing neighborhood, but I saw nothing too ominous.

As we drove through the winding streets of the territories, I kept trying to read the Arabic graffiti. It was difficult to decipher. At one point, Ilan pointed to a red streak of graffiti that said: "If you are driving through this neighborhood and you are loyal to Hamas, turn the lights on inside your car now."

Such are the ploys Hamas uses to ensure the loyalty of their neighborhoods. A crude but effective tactic, in keeping with the style of terrorist organizations like Hamas, Fatah, and Islamic Jihad, which rule through blunt intimidation and fear. From the front of the van, Boaz radioed to the unmarked Peugeot and confirmed that they had switched on their interior light. Ilan let out a sardonic laugh. "You know what's funny?" he said. "Look, they even spelled the word 'neighborhood' wrong."

As we approached the drop-off point, we heard honking horns and general chaos. The road ahead was closed: a minor car accident or overturned food cart and everything was backed up. Ilan and Boaz consulted the aerial photograph, ordering a fast detour to get us back on track. All of a sudden, I started to appreciate the complexity of the variables, all the things you couldn't learn in the classroom or on the firing range, how fast things change in the field.

Three blocks from the target, we piled out of the van and proceeded to run down the block in groups of twos and threes.

My assignment was to take up a post on one of the corners, facing the building to be taken, but being mindful of my rear at the same time. My primary responsibility was to make sure that the entry-and-extraction team—B Team—had a clear path to the front door and that they didn't get shot at en route. If any Palestinian popped up in a window with a gun or threw a grenade, I would shout, "Stop! Pull back!" But then I had orders to engage, returning fire with the combatants.

We cordoned off the neighborhood. I looked up at our snipers and spotters, moving into position on the rooftops. I knew we could be shot at from any direction. I was carrying a rocket-propelled grenade launcher—or "RPG"—as well as a Negev machine gun. We were making a tremendous show of firepower, just in case something went wrong.

B-Team hit the door, entered, and swept the house. Within minutes they ascertained that our prime target* wasn't there, but they radioed that they were snatching up a secondary target, a cousin of our main target, who was also on the wanted list. B Team left with the suspect in cuffs, and then our canine unit entered the house with German shepherds, to sniff out hidden guns and explosives.

The whole mission was over in minutes, unfolding perfectly, like a coordinated ballet. No shots fired. No injuries to either side. Everything went off without a hitch, and except for the fact that we missed the primary target and had to settle for a secondary, it would have been a textbook mission.

B Team led the captured Palestinian toward us. His hands were

---

* Target's name redacted for security reasons.

pinned behind his back with flex-cuffs, and his eyes were covered with a strip of white felt. We marched him to the van and bundled him inside. He wasn't struggling or shaking. He didn't say a word to us during the whole drive out of the territories. And no one on our team talked in front of him. When we got back to the base, two agents from Shabak were waiting in the debriefing room. We turned the suspect over to Shabak for interrogation. We never saw him again.

An hour later, during the debriefing, Ilan and Boaz went around the room, critiquing us all in turn. No mission is perfect; there are always techniques we could have improved. Mostly, the officers were concerned with how we'd adapted to the changing realities of the mission. Right at the outset, as one of our snipers had jogged from one roof to another to get a better angle, the rest of us had to adjust our positions accordingly. At another point, the officers had pulled one of the guys from my perimeter element because they needed another person on the entry element. Some of us hadn't reacted smoothly enough; we'd been too stiff, too preprogrammed. So the main debriefing from that mission was to think better on your feet.

"Guys," Ilan said, "you've got to be ready to change on the fly. Don't be a fucking robot. We told you to do X and Y, but be ready to do Z. You're *thinking* here. You have to improvise."

I would do that same mission, over and over again during my service, at least a hundred times. Different towns, different streets, different targets. The only thing that changed was my role in the mission. As the months went by, I was moved up to increasingly more significant positions. When we rammed the door, or took it down with an explosive charge, I would be the second or third guy on the entry team, storming inside, machine gun leveled, shouting: *"Jesh! Jesh!"*

And that's when things turned hot. That's when I started doing a lot of shooting.

EIGHTEEN

The heart and soul, or perhaps I should say the brains, of our unit is the central operations room. It constantly reeks of cigarette smoke because every officer chain-smokes. The tables and chairs are cheap, ugly, with wobbly legs and chipped corners, like something out of a Jewish day school. The floor is nondescript linoleum, clean-swept but scuffed from the black rubber soles of combat boots and New Balance sneakers. The adrenaline is constantly flowing, as is the black coffee.

A never-ending cycle of missions is planned and executed in that room. Every single mission is an attempt to take down a terrorist leader. We're not after the suicide bombers, but rather the planners and fund-raisers, the command-and-control of groups like Hamas, Hezbollah, and Islamic Jihad. We zero in on the moneymen and their assistants, the explosives experts and bomb builders, the people who provide the safe houses and store the equipment, right down to the lowly runners and couriers who pass along information. The suicide bomber, the man, woman, or child who actually commits the terrorist act, knows very little about the crime itself. The planners don't tell the bombers anything.

They are little more than brainwashed pawns—mostly lost young men manipulated into turning themselves into human bombs. It makes no sense for Duvdevan to take down some sixteen- or seventeen-year-old kid who's been recruited in the mosque. By and large, our list of targets contains roughly two hundred names at any given time, and as we snatch one or two men, the list is always refreshed with new faces and names. On one wall of the operations room are taped-up photographs of all the guys we're currently going after; on the other side of the room hang photos of all the guys we've already nabbed or killed during missions.

The ethic in the unit, as in all the Israeli Special Forces branches, is to work without emotion. We aren't the soul-searching, morally tortured Mossad operatives depicted in Steven Spielberg's *Munich*. Nor are we sociopathic hit men or trigger-happy cowboys.

Emotions are nothing but a liability during an operation. They cloud your judgment and get you and your teammates killed. Clinical, cold-eyed detachment is required for this kind of effort. If during your extensive background checks, the IDF finds out that you've lost a loved one—even a distant family member—in a terrorist attack, you're not allowed to serve in a combat unit. Every effort is made to weed out soldiers whose judgment may be blinded by a thirst for vengeance.

Our commanding officer in the unit was Colonel Muki, the stocky little thirty-six-year-old colonel who had bowled us all over in Krav Maga during basic training. But most of the orders came directly from Captain Zoar. Zoar was a young no-nonsense officer, in charge of two teams of Duvdevan. Raised in south Tel Aviv, muscular, Sephardic, about twenty-six years old, Zoar had a deadpan expression, dry wit, and soft-spoken demeanor.

From our first meeting, Zoar really took a liking to me. He loved that I was a fish out of water; he saw me as a younger version of Ilan, only instead of being a blue-eyed, blond-haired Aussie, I was a crazy Canadian transplant from Beverly Hills. I was only a month into being fully operational when Zoar gave me my first big undercover role. That morning there were several teams, about forty men, gathered in the operations room.

"Listen," Zoar said. "Shabak intercepted a phone call last night. They've positively identified the voice as Dr. Ibrahim Fahdi. Right now, he's ranked as the number-three guy in Hamas. He's a money guy, a fund-raiser. He's clever and very elusive. We've already missed him a bunch of times. We know he's staying right now at a hotel in East Jerusalem."

This was a problem. Working in East Jerusalem meant we couldn't safely attempt a standard Duvdevan operation. Even in Arab disguise, we'd be instantly recognized as outsiders.

"*Mista'aravim* isn't an option this time," Zoar continued. "You've all been in East Jerusalem during training. You all know that quarter is too close, the streets are too narrow and tight. The shopkeepers and vendors know everyone and see everything. It's a neighborhood of ten thousand spies. We need to do something unconventional this time, throw the playbook out the window."

He nodded at me across the table.

"Aaron, tonight you're gonna get some peroxide. You're gonna bleach your hair. You're gonna shave and you're gonna put in your earrings."

"Okay."

There were a few smirks around the operations room.

"You'll be a journalist from the States. You'll be yourself—an American kid from Los Angeles. We're gonna set up an interview in East Jerusalem with Dr. Fahdi. If we can get him to meet you, it'll be in a public place, in a restaurant or café. We'll have eyeballs on you at all times. You'll be surrounded. You're gonna engage him there for an hour, act as a diversion only, and then initiate the takedown."

That night I bleached my hair and shaved my face. The next morning we took photos and made up fake press credentials and some other ID. I was supposed to be a hip, young journalist, straight out of UCLA, now a staff writer for the *Jerusalem Post*. I was doing a freelance piece, a feature on the Palestinians' political aims.

The meeting with Dr. Fahdi was set for three days later, at a tiny joint called the Palestine Café in the old quarter . Our reconnaissance team had surveilled the café well, and followed Dr. Fahdi's movements in and out of his hotel for the past twelve hours. I got to the Palestine Café before he did and sat at a corner table, trying not to show my state of anxiety. It was a chilly night but I could feel the sweat beading on my forehead. After months of hard-core Special Forces living, I felt ludicrous in my civilian disguise, sitting in the ancient city of David, with my bleached-blond hair and down-filled ski vest and baggy Diesel jeans. Suddenly, I was no longer an elite warrior;

I was just some skate-punk poseur from the San Fernando Valley. I fidgeted with my spiral notepad and pen and placed my professional-quality Sony recorder on the table.

In case Fahdi's bodyguards wanted to frisk me, the only weapon I could have on me was a small-caliber handgun, a slim .22 Beretta, tucked deep by the ankle in my boot.

I reminded myself that the teams of warriors surrounding me were among the best trained in the world. The three members of the first team were seated nearby in a coffee shop, pretending to be European tourists, looking at a map of the city. Across the narrow street, there was a three-man sniper team set up on the roof by the Dome of the Rock. And there was an excellent, small cell of guys for the takedown: all dark-skinned Sephardic commandos, pretending to be Border Patrol soldiers, dressed in distinctive, short-sleeve, dark green uniforms with blue shoulder patches. The Border Patrol units, drawn primarily from the Sephardim, are commonplace in the Arab quarter of Jerusalem and our takedown guys would draw no undue attention.

I had a tiny earbud receiver deep inside my ear canal, and the signal for the takedown was a double-click.

About a quarter past six, Dr. Fahdi arrived with three bodyguards. He smiled and shook my hand firmly. His bodyguards stared daggers but they didn't pat me down. Fahdi called to the waiter in Arabic to bring him a coffee. I stuck with my glass of water. He was a paunchy man, in his mid-forties, salt-and-pepper hair at his temples. He was polite and spoke fluent English with an educated British accent. He'd received a doctorate in economics somewhere in the U.K.

I started to ask him about his political goals, but then I completely lost my concentration. I wasn't worried about the hand-to-hand skills of Fahdi's bodyguards; I was confident my own Krav Maga would take them out if it came to a struggle. What worried me was their erratic temperament. I'd often heard that the actions of Hamas bodyguards were impossible to anticipate. They might sit calmly; they might just as easily freak out, kill you without a millisecond's warning. Something might spook them, a stray cat jumping from a wall, and they'd shoot you in the face just to be on the safe side. I glanced at the three bodyguards, stern-faced, with neat mustaches, all wearing sports shirts, sipping their little cups of Turkish coffee.

It wasn't just the bodyguards that worried me. This professor was a bigwig from Hamas, which meant the streets were full of fanatics who would kill for him in a heartbeat. The whole neighborhood would swarm down on us like hornets. Snipers or no snipers, if the operation went south, I could easily get stabbed by some street vendor in the mayhem.

But slowly, my concentration returned and I fell into an interviewing groove. I saw the beauty of the reporter's cover Zoar had chosen for me. Whenever I felt uneasy, I could shut up and let Fahdi do the talking. I'd ask him a gentle, probing question about the Palestinian cause, then nod intently and take notes, periodically checking my tape recorder.

Somehow we ended up talking for over two hours. I'd filled a dozen pages of notes and had to pop in a new cassette. I was forming a strong, genuine connection with the professor. It began as an act—I needed to seem sympathetic because I needed him to believe me—but then it changed into something else.

This was the one danger I hadn't anticipated, an inevitable pitfall of undercover work. When you get into character, really playing your role, you start *connecting* with your target. He's not some two-dimensional bad guy you've been surveilling; he's a flesh-and-blood man, with kids in college, and a prostate condition. You listen to him speaking passionately about the plight of the Palestinian people, and on some level—even though you know better intellectually—your emotional side begins to see the world through his eyes.

And Fahdi was a wonderful speaker. His precise BBC English was mesmerizing and his meandering sentences, perfectly tossed at me like looping coils of rope, were hypnotic.

When I got the double-click in my earbud, I couldn't instantly disengage. I completely froze for a couple of seconds. But my expression must've changed because Fahdi paused, midsentence, staring hard. Then his slate gray eyes narrowed with unease.

The team double-clicked again, and then a third time.

I cleared the cobwebs from my mind, stared hard at Fahdi's forehead, and remembered the face of the fourteen-year-old girl with the smudged costume makeup and the singed hula skirt whose pulse grew fainter as I pressed her cold lips to mine back at the Dizengoff Mall.

I jumped across the table and punched Fahdi in the face as hard as I could. With that one punch I could tell I'd busted his fucking nose in three pieces; blood was spurting everywhere. I hit him in the mouth, and felt his teeth loosen, and a sharp pain shot from my fist up my forearm. I drew my Beretta from inside my boot and started smashing him in the head with my gun. I was beating the shit out of him so intensely, so in the zone, that I barely realized that my backup guys were beating the shit out of the bodyguards.

The takedown unit rushed in and started firing a bunch of shots into the wall and floor, just to freak everyone out and scatter the bystanders. I remember our Border Patrol guys coming in with German shepherds and the snipers jumping down from their positions on the mosque. I was still beating Fahdi with my gun when they pulled him away, threw him into one of the Border Patrol jeeps, and got him out of the Arab quarter and into the hands of Shabak interrogators. The takedown was flawless, over in about half a minute. It wasn't until I was back at the base that I realized the blood all over my white shirt and Diesel jeans was not all Dr. Fahdi's. As I was washing, I saw a wide, bloody gash above my right hand knuckles from when my fist connected with his teeth. It was a deep cut and took fifteen stitches to close.

NINETEEN

Eventually, you start to get comfortable with your fear. As you gain a better sense of the Palestinian neighborhoods you're going into over and over, you become more at ease with the work. It's a feeling you have to diligently fight against. Becoming too comfortable is the most dangerous state to be in as an undercover operator.

My hand was still on the mend from the Palestine Café mission when Zoar gave me a valuable piece of advice. I was confiding in him about the nauseating nervousness I'd felt waiting for the takedown with Dr. Fahdi.

"Good, Aaron. Don't lose that feeling. Don't get numb. Don't ever stop being afraid. The moment you stop being afraid is the moment you'll get taken by surprise."

I knew from my first few missions that the adrenaline rush of going into the field could make the new soldiers a little overzealous.

We had to hone that state of razor-sharp alertness that accompanies fear while not making the mistakes of being overanxious, impatient, or trigger-happy.

As I started to process what we were doing day to day, I realized that no matter how accurate the intelligence from Shabak, or how carefully the mission was planned, how straight I might shoot, there were so many variables in every operation that I could never be prepared enough. My awareness during missions became so acute as to be overdeveloped; I was so hyper-conscious of 360 degrees of sensory perceptions that it began to feel like an intense form of paranoia.

As the weeks progressed, that self-protective paranoia forced me into a zone where I became very quiet. I stopped talking about the missions, even after-hours playing *shesh-besh* with Inon or Dedi or Ilan. We'd all stopped talking about the work. Within a month, we had come to accept this state of emotional insulation as a byproduct of working in one of the world's most dangerous jobs.

The most dangerous missions were those where we didn't have the luxury of going out at two or three o'clock in the morning. The middle of the night is always the most advantageous operating time, since there's much less likelihood of a shoot-out or widespread neighborhood unrest when the majority of people are sacked out. But there are times when the real-time intel is such that we have no choice but to go out at seven in the evening, for example, during the middle of dinner. The moment our takedown team hits the neighborhood, people start spreading the word, waving their arms and screaming Arabic warnings up and down the blocks.

"Jesh, jesh, jesh!" they'll shout. Or they'll say, *"Jesh wissech!"* which means "the stinking army" in Arabic. And from the moment those words ring out, all bets are off.

Almost all Palestinian neighborhoods are gang-held territories, like sections of Chicago during the Al Capone era, or L.A. today under the thumb of the Crips and Bloods. The only distinction in the West Bank is that the two principal gangs are called Hamas and Fatah. It's too dignified to call them "movements" because however organized they are, however much they cloak themselves in a veil of righteous political, religious, and nationalist rhetoric, these groups operate with the mentality of street thugs. They're gangsters and killers. They're the worst kind of bullies, preying on their own population.

The way they recruit new members is insidious. They'll go up to some sixteen- or seventeen-year-old kid, just as he's leaving school or the mosque.

"Are you with us?" they ask.

"Of course I'm with you!"

"Then prove it."

And how do they ask him to prove it? They give him a vest loaded with explosives and nails and tell him to go blow himself up in a crowd of Israeli civilians. What can the kid do? If he refuses outright, they'll kill him. If he seems frightened and hesitates before agreeing, they'll think he's a snitch for the Israelis and kill him. The only way he can preserve his honor and protect his family is to wear the suicide bomb for these gangster bosses.

It's the tyranny of terror. The neighborhoods are so thoroughly controlled by the gangs that everyone knows every vehicle that comes in and out. Once we are in takedown mode, we've got at most three minutes to get set up, make entry into the house, and snatch that target, or we'll have a gigantic clusterfuck on our hands.

Even if our cover isn't blown, it's extraordinary how fast things can go bad. One early evening, Shabak had contacted us about a dangerous high-ranking character from Hamas who'd been holed up in a safe house in Jenin for weeks. The terrorist warrant on this guy was truly frightening. A terrorist warrant is a highly classified document produced by the Shabak and sent to the unit, containing extraordinarily detailed research about past crimes, affiliations, hideouts, and aliases. Unlike an American police warrant, a suspect is never shown this document, nor is it used in court in any way. No one outside of Shabak and the Duvdevan team ever sees it. The warrant contains every bit of information relevant to our successfully taking the suspect into custody for interrogation. For example, I remember one warrant that warned us that a particular terrorist was an eighth-degree black belt in karate, a useful fact to know when you're preparing to corner a man in his own house.

The warrant for the Hamas big shot hiding in Jenin indicated that he had personally been responsible for several lethal attacks on IDF soldiers. He also had a history of ambushing Israeli tanks and armored vehicles and taking shots at rank-and-file IDF men on patrol. His weapon of choice was an AK-47.

The target was so high-risk that the commanders wanted two teams from Duvdevan, two teams from the Border Patrol, and one team from Matkal working in conjunction on the mission.

We'd rendezvoused with the Border Patrol and the Matkal near Tel Aviv so were starting out from within Israel proper. This was highly unusual since the Duvdevan base itself is located within the Palestinian-held territories, meaning we don't usually have to pass through any checkpoints when going after targets in cities like Jenin, Ramallah, Hebron, or Jericho.

But during this mission, we had to enter Jenin in full *mista'aravim* mode, driving three Arab cars, all decked out with authentic blue Palestinian Authority plates. I was riding in a beat-up 1983 Peugeot, dressed up as a young Palestinian, wearing a red-and-white keffiyeh wrapped over my head and full beard.

Leaving Israel, we were flying past columns of the Israeli army who were on routine maneuvers, and then the traffic slowed to a crawl, backed up for over an hour to get through the checkpoint. Then this one fucking Golani soldier, casually strolling past with his rifle, decided to stare into our window and ask a bunch of questions.

This presented us with a massive dilemma: We couldn't tell the regular army what we were up to without compromising our cover. All of us were carrying Palestinian ID papers. It would be near impossible to talk our way out of any jam without jeopardizing the mission.

The hard-on from Golani gestured for our Peugeot to pull over. What the hell was he doing? Singling us out as potential terrorists? We were supposedly Palestinian civilians crossing back into the Arab side—the IDF never stops the cars going in *that* direction. We were pretending to be day laborers returning to homes in the West Bank. (After the outbreak of the Second Intifada, the government has stopped allowing Palestinian day workers to come so freely into Israel.)

If the Golani infantryman ordered us out of the car and detained us on suspicion of being terrorists, it would not only compromise our cover, it would blow the whole mission—the other Duvdevan team, the Matkal team, and the Border Patrol would arrive in Jenin, find themselves woefully undermanned, and have to abort the takedown. Just then, Zoar, our officer, pulled a trump card. He called the Golani soldier close to the window and with an irate expression, in a very low whisper, he began speaking in Hebrew—with an accent and ball-breaking military intonation no Palestinian, no matter how skilled, was likely to ever pull off.

"Listen to me closely, soldier. We're on a pre-cleared mission to get a target in Jenin. You're interfering with us getting to that target—a high-priority terrorist warrant. You understand?"

Zoar then flipped open a secret compartment in the car—one I'd never seen before or been taught to use—and removed an authentic IDF captain's identification. Zoar cupped it carefully in one hand, flashed it for just a second, and returned it to its hiding place.

The poor Golani infantryman backed away from the car, eyes wide and darting, speechless over the world of trouble his routine car stop had almost kicked off. He raised his rifle and waved us through the checkpoint. Our driver hit the gas, proceeding into the crowded streets of Jenin.

About a kilometer from the safe house we jumped out of the Peugeot and walked through a swarming market. We broke into pairs, stationed ourselves at various corners of the marketplace, and tried to keep a low profile, strolling and smoking cigarettes for about thirty minutes. We kept the safe house under close surveillance the whole time. We radioed back to command that we believed the target was still inside.

We casually returned to our undercover cars and drove out of visual range, then switched cars, getting into the three takedown vans, stripping off our undercover disguises and strapping on our guns and gear. When we were about a block from the safe house, we exited the vans, our heads and faces covered by black hoods and balaklavas.

"Take the door," came the order over the radios.

We began to knock loudly, shouting:

"Jesh! Jesh!"

There was no response from inside and we were just about to breach the door with battering rams when we heard the report of an assault rifle. From the sound, we instantly recognized it as a Kalashnikov. We all turned, disoriented, confused as to the position of the gunman. We heard more bursts from the AK. Zoar and Ilan turned, crouching low, frantically pointing to the second floor of the house across the street. We backed away from the gunfire, taking cover against the walls of the safe house. I'm asking myself, *What do I do? What do I do? The whole operation is going haywire.* I raised the barrel of my short M-16 to return the fire, but didn't get off a single round. Zoar had decided to order another, more devastating response.

"Udi! Udi!" he called.

There was one guy in the unit nicknamed Udi Lawi. His real name was Udi Levi, but everyone called him Udi Lawi because he was an incredible shot with the M72-LAW—or light antitank weapon—a tubelike single-shot 66-mm armor-piercing rocket.

More assault rifle bursts came from the second-story window across the lane. A few of the shots ricocheted in the concrete a few feet in front of us.

"Udi," Zoar said calmly. "Give him one LAW."

Udi stepped forward and took aim. With a high-pitched whoosh, the LAW rocket shot straight through the open window. After a moment, we saw a huge flare of fire, heard screaming, and the gunfire ceased.

We stormed into the house, sweeping all the rooms and floors methodically. When we got to the second story we located the Hamas target we'd been hunting for—sprawled on the floor, still clutching his AK-47. He was charred almost beyond recognition. The curtains and carpeting in the room were still smoldering.

That is real-time counterterrorist work in the territories. We planned to take the safe house and bring the suspect back to Shabak for interrogation. Instead, we came under fire from an AK-47. Knowing the suspect had fired on—and killed—IDF soldiers in the past, Zoar and Ilan didn't hesitate in their response. The moment the threat to our safety was deemed lethal, they ordered an end to the firefight with one crushing display of LAW rocket firepower.

It didn't take me long to recognize the fundamental paradox of our work. How do you capture a wanted man whose belief system tells him *never* to be captured alive? Many of our targets would rather shoot it out and die in a blaze of glory than be marched back to our Shabak interrogators in handcuffs.

Our goal was always to achieve a peaceful surrender. Whenever we surrounded the perimeter of a house, we used a 180-degree approach, coming through one main door, while guns from operators on the perimeter were focused on all possible points of exit. Then one of two things would happen: we would knock on the door, announcing ourselves to be the Israeli army and ordering the occupants to come outside, or else a demolition expert would put a small charge on the door and blow it off its hinges.

We would always prefer to use the former method; explosives and gunplay increase the odds of fatality on both sides. The whole reason the unit was created during the First Intifada—the entire methodology behind our training—was to take our targets alive. Simply put: The terrorist leaders and masterminds are no good to us as corpses. We want the information they can provide to our Shabak interrogation team. On every mission, we're determined not to use lethal force unless it's necessary.

That being said, the moment our team is at risk, the gloves come off. We are authorized to kill any terrorists trying to kill a member of our team. We have orders to shoot at couches, behind televisions, at refrigerators and washing machines, pouring bullets into any corner of the house where an assailant could be hiding.

The philosophy lies at the core of the nation's defensive policy regarding its Arab neighbors, an uncompromising sentiment most famously defined in a 1955 speech by then-IDF Chief of Staff Moshe Dayan. "We cannot protect every water pipe from being blown up, nor every tree from being uprooted," Dayan said. "Nor can we prevent the murder of the workers in the orchards, nor of families in their beds, but we *can exact a high price for our blood*, a price too high for the Arab community, the Arab army, the Arab governments to pay."

Most of the guys in the unit, especially the more seasoned operators like Ilan, would grow heated whenever civilian pundits started debating the rationale behind employing such seemingly disproportionate responses to Palestinian violence.

"They accuse us of being a unit of assassins," I remember a guy from one of the other teams telling me one night in the barracks, referring to reports in the left-wing Israeli press as well as in some European newspapers about Duvdevan. "Yeah, what a crock of shit! It's the terrorist bastards who'd rather die than be taken alive. I'm supposed to compromise my safety because some scumbag terrorist is too proud to surrender? Because he'd rather be a martyr than be taken into custody? If he wants to go to Allah so bad, no problem. I'll help him get there. I will piggyback him up to Allah personally. You want your seventy-two virgins in Paradise, come on, let's go! *Kadimah!*"

Those words may sound hotheaded to non-Israelis—that was just the intensity of his personality—but in essence, we all came to agree wholeheartedly with the sentiment. We were faced on a daily basis in the territories with a mentality of such murderous recklessness that, in order to safeguard the lives of our fellow teammates, we had no choice but to respond in the most aggressive and often lethal manner possible.

Unlike many American Special Forces units and civilian SWAT teams, the Israeli counterterrorism method for clearing a target location is cautious and deliberate. To American eyes, it might look ridiculously slow-motion. But there's an entire protocol for sweeping 90-degree angles and hallways. When it's executed properly, it's like a choreographed dance, everyone knowing exactly where they're supposed to be, and the overlapping coordination between the operators is perfect. It's a slow-tempo dance done with short-barreled M-16s and bulletproof vests.

Why move so slowly? The Israeli theory is that if there are no hostages, then why run? What's the rush? Unless there a confirmed hostage situation, our methodology is to move as deliberately as we can. Even during training, if a guy was a little too gung-ho to move forward, the instructor would scream at him: "What's your hurry? Do you want to die quicker?"

American Special Forces units like the Navy SEALs, Green Berets, Army Rangers, as well as many police SWAT teams are taught to think completely differently about making such clearances. Their whole philosophy is to make a "dynamic entry." What that means, in practice, is coming in as hard and as fast and with as many men as you can—overwhelming the suspect with speed and firepower. Israel CT teams have learned, the hard way, that "dynamic clears" often result in a lot of unnecessary casualties, a lot of friendly-fire deaths.

When we are about to clear a house, we let the targets know that we are coming in no uncertain terms. Roughly six times out of seven, if the target has a weapon, we will come under fire. And once he fires, we start throwing grenades. Then we'll withdraw from the house. Sometimes we'll send our canine unit in; if the dogs don't return, then we'll call in an army bulldozer and level the house, flat as a pancake. But in most of our missions it's such a high-priority warrant, such a valuable target, that we need to take every practical measure to capture him alive.

A suspect never fires on us because he thinks he has a chance of escaping. He fires on us because he wants to die. He'd rather be a martyr than end up in an Israeli jail cell, being interrogated by Shabak agents. It's a disgrace within the Arab community to be taken alive. Suspects usually prefer to shoot it out and die with dignity.

The violence we faced was rarely the sort where a terrorist pulls out a pistol and decides to fire on us face-to-face, like a modern-day O.K. Corral. During my tour in the territories, we were usually attacked in the form of ambushes and blindsides, with our team coming under a barrage from unseen kids holed up in the neighborhood, or anonymous Hamas or Fatah gunmen acting as the enforcers for the block.

The moment they started gunning, we had orders to pull the plug on the mission and start gunning in return. Most of the time we'd be shooting on the run or from the window of a speeding vehicle. I'll never forget the first time I fired my short-barreled M-16 (without benefit of the earplugs used during training) out the window of an undercover car. Nothing prepared me for the report of an M-16 in a confined vehicle. It was literally deafening: I had a high-pitched whistling in my ears for three days after the mission.

In the territories, everyone is a potential attacker—old men with canes, women carrying groceries, little kids kicking beat-up soccer balls. An attack can come from any direction. Every window on every block hides a potential gunman; every hallway and corner a potentially lethal blade. One night, around ten P.M., we were executing a terrorist warrant in Jenin. A middle-aged woman, wearing traditional Palestinian dress with a head scarf, answered the door. She was quiet and demure. She looked like a typical mother.

"Where's Ahmed?" I said in Arabic.

"Ahmed's not here," she said.

"You're sure? We're going to come inside this house and God forbid anyone's hiding here."

We started moving through the house with our canine unit and I made the mistake of letting the woman out of my sight for a millisecond. Suddenly, she popped up in my peripheral vision again, coming at me from the kitchen with a long knife, screaming in Arabic, swinging the knife at me.

I started reacting without thinking—the Krav Maga aggressiveness training was entirely hard-wired into me. The knife sliced at my hand once, then twice, as I was blocking her swings, pushing her backward and off-balance. Still the blade kept slicing down at a blinding pace. Finally I took the butt of my rifle and struck her square on the chin, splitting it wide open, blood gushing everywhere.

She fell to the ground, not unconscious but dazed, and as I backed away into the hallway I realized I was covered not only in her blood but mine too, spurting and dripping on the floor. She had managed to catch me cleanly just below my wrist, shredding the fabric of my gloves. The wound was gushing hard, but there was so much adrenaline rushing through me, that I hadn't even felt the cut.

No matter how much I tried to mentally prepare myself before missions, such blindsides were always a hazard of the job. It happened even when my unit found ourselves in the unusual position of having to turn our guns on our fellow Jews.

There's no denying the fact that extremism exists on both sides of the religious divide. Of course, I have little patience for anti-Zionist propaganda that sees Israel's defensive action as equivalent to Palestinian aggression. But once you've done a military tour in the territories—or "Judea and Samaria," as the Zionist settlers always refer to them—you can't escape the fact that some of our Jewish extremists can be nearly as irrational as the Palestinian fanatics.

In Hebron I got my first taste of hard-core American-born settlers. It caught me unaware—a sucker punch from the heart of Brooklyn.

Hebron has always been a powder keg, its history written in rivers of blood. The ancient town is sacred to both Muslims and Jews, and it's the location of the Tomb of the Patriarchs—known to Jews as the Me'arat HaMachpela and to Muslims as the Ibrahimi Mosque or Sanctuary of Abraham—believed to be the burial site of Abraham, Isaac, and Jacob. During the infamous Hebron Massacre of 1929, the Arab population, spurred on by inflammatory speeches by the Grand Mufti in Jerusalem, attacked the tiny Jewish community (numbering some eight hundred) that had been living in the town of ten thousand Muslims undisturbed for many years. In all, some sixty-seven Jews were murdered in the summer of 1929.

One of the worst massacres in the post–Oslo Accords period was perpetrated in Hebron by an Orthodox Jewish fanatic. Known as the "Cave of the Patriarchs Massacre," the horrific slaughter has often been called a key factor in destabilizing the Palestinians' trust in the peace process. On February 25, 1994, an American-born Orthodox settler, Baruch Goldstein, a physician by training (he'd studied at Albert Einstein College of Medicine in New York) and a follower of the controversial rabbi Meir Kahane, entered the mosque of the Cave of the Patriarchs wearing the green uniform of an IDF reservist. He opened fire with a Galil assault rifle, instantly killing 29 Muslim worshippers and wounding 150. After being subdued with a fire extinguisher and disarmed, Goldstein was beaten to death by the mob.

Early in my Duvdevan tour, Hebron once again erupted in violent chaos. The unrest was sparked by the unexpected arrival of Ariel Sharon. Sharon wasn't the opposition leader at the time; he was a man in the wilderness, having lost the Likud leadership race to Bibi Netanyahu. His visit to Hebron was seen as a political ploy to outhawk the hawkish Bibi. As with his visit to Jerusalem's Temple Mount, the mere news that Sharon—nicknamed the "Bulldozer" for his penchant for advocating the wholesale leveling of Palestinian neighborhoods suspected of fomenting terrorism—was setting foot in Hebron set off unrest among the Palestinians. Soon there was widespread fighting between the Muslim majority and the small but fanatical enclave of ultra-Orthodox settlers.

I was on a team sent to assist the regular IDF soldiers who were forcibly moving the settlers. The Orthodox Jews were positioned on an embankment near the holy shrine Sharon had visited, refusing our direct orders to move from the hillside.

The American-born settlers were shouting at me in Hebrew:

"How can you do this? We are *Jews*! This is *Jewish* land! You should be ashamed!"

I felt ambivalent leveling my gun at the Jewish settlers—I didn't sign up to point my gun at Jews—but I had my orders.

"Move along! Move along!" I shouted, gesturing with my M-16.

Without warning, a crazed kerchief-wearing woman rushed at me. She was screaming in Hebrew with a distinctly Brooklyn accent. Over and over, she called me a traitor. She got close enough that I could smell her breath. The spittle was flying. I stood my ground.

Then she punched me in the face. Operating on pure reflex and Krav Maga training, I caught her with an elbow strike to the jaw, using the butt of my short-barreled M-16 as an extension of my elbow's power. She collapsed to the ground, dazed, weeping, bleeding from the chin.

I stood over her, explaining to her in English why I'd struck her with my M-16.

"I'm just doing my job," I said. "We've got orders to clear the embankment and that's what we're going to do. I didn't mean to hurt you, lady, but you shouldn't have hit me. I'm an Israeli soldier. I'm not a traitor. Believe me, this isn't an easy assignment for any of us. But we do have direct orders to follow. Now clear the embankment!"

As she staggered back to her feet, the look of fanatical hatred in her eyes remained undiminished.

My first fatal engagement occurred during one of our largest operations in Jenin. We were hunting a major Hamas target, a young Palestinian who'd already spent time in an Israeli jail for acts of terrorism, been released, and was now back at work as a Hamas terror planner. He was holed up somewhere in Jenin, and we had terrorist warrants on him and his first cousin and an uncle. We had more than our usual number of teams on the mission, plus regular IDF for backup, which was unusual for Duvdevan. The command had clearly assessed that there was a high risk the target would resist with lethal force.

We weren't working undercover on this one; we were in door-kicking mode. We came in through the back streets of the territories, driving to our designated target and, jumping out about a half mile from our destination, continued on foot. With close to 150 guys on that mission, we shut down an entire block.

Our plan required that we hit several addresses at the same time, because we didn't know which house the primary and secondary targets were hiding in. It was the first time I'd been on an operation executing multiple terrorist warrants simultaneously.

I was assigned to the secondary target house where we believed the uncle, also known to have planned terror operations, had been living. The building was so large that we needed fifteen guys on my entry team. We knew that there would be family members inside, many innocent women and children, and we didn't want to go inside with guns blazing.

We hit them early, about seven in the evening. We banged on the door, shouting in Arabic.

"*Jesh! Jesh! Iftah el-bab!* Army, Army! Open up now!"

The door didn't open. We banged again.

"*Jesh! Jesh!* Open up or we're taking the door down!"

We heard movement inside and we got the command to breach the door. It was a massive, solid metal door that could not be battered by conventional means. One of our operators jumped out of a van with a welding torch. We set up protective cover while he went to work with the torch melting down the hinges.

As soon as the sparks finished flying, and we removed the front door, an older, stoop-shouldered man emerged. It later turned out that he was yet another cousin of the main Hamas target. He told us the house was empty, that no one was inside except him.

Ilan shot him a skeptical glare, got several inches from his face, barking: "Is there anyone inside the house we need to know about?"

"No one, no one!"

We covered the man's face, put plastic handcuffs on him, and took him to one of our vans.

We stormed through the front door to sweep the vast building.

There were four floors, and numerous staircases and hallways, a lot of square footage to clear effectively. I was working with Zoar and three of my teammates, including Dedi and Yossi. We were communicating back and forth constantly by radio. Dedi and I were working in tandem, which is protocol when clearing a series of rooms. Dedi entered an empty living room, then lurched back. We heard movement coming from behind the battered beige couch. The space was too tight for me to use my M-4 effectively. I felt I couldn't maneuver properly, so I drew my Sig Sauer pistol. Dedi and I were both shouting in Arabic.

"Jesh! Jesh! Ta'al la-hon! Put your hands in the air!"

Suddenly, a teenage kid bolted from behind the sofa with a pistol in his hand.

"Jesh! Jesh!" we screamed, raising our guns.

The kid aimed the pistol—a cheap, banged-up-looking Soviet-era 9-mm—and fired, hitting the door behind me, the bullet ricocheting past my helmet.

In a flash both Dedi and I opened fire. We hit the Palestinian kid at least six times. One of my shots struck him squarely between the eyes. He collapsed to the floor.

Zoar was just a few feet behind me, slowly sweeping the room to ensure there were no other gunmen. He glanced down at the dead teenager, then threw a fluorescent lightstick into the room to let the other teams know we'd made the clear.

Our radios began squawking in unison:

"There's shooting coming from some of our guys! Back room, northeast corner! Everybody has permission to begin firing on every room!"

Now every member of the entry team lit up every room. The

sound of the simultaneous M-4 and M-16 gunfire was something I'll never forget, like apocalyptic typewriters, reverberating from the walls of that building like they'd never stop.

Back at the base, two Shabak agents informed me that the mission had been a success. We had captured the primary target—the Hamas planner who'd done time in an Israeli prison—as well as his uncle. Both were in Shabak hands now, being interrogated. The kid I'd killed, they said, was only fifteen years old.

"He was a known courier for Hamas," one of the agents said. "He'd been running messages and errands for them for years."

After the Shabak agents left, I sat there alone in the debriefing room, smoking cigarette after cigarette, not wanting to talk to anyone else. It was a tough night: Known Hamas courier or not, this wasn't what I enlisted for. I didn't sign up to kill kids.

After the fatal shooting, as the Israeli Special Forces regulations mandate, I was pulled out of operations for a month. I was put into temporary operational limbo, allowed to continue training but not to engage in further missions.

I had to explain the incident multiple times, first in a debriefing at the command post in the field, then in the debriefing room at the unit base, then with the interviewers from Shabak who asked me to describe the shooting over and over in minute detail. They wanted to make certain that my decision to use lethal force was justified, that it wasn't done with malicious intent, and it wasn't an execution. They wanted to confirm that I had been in fear for my life and for the lives of my teammates.

The next morning, first thing, I was ordered to report to the army psychiatrist. The psychiatrist was a decent guy—youngish, in his early thirties. He'd been the doctor who gave us our physical exams throughout our time in the unit and I'd gotten to know him socially. Now I had to see him every two days to talk about my psychological and emotional state.

Over and over, I described what happened. The whole firefight had lasted no more than three or four seconds; I'd now been talking about it for at least that many hours.

"Are you okay with your actions?" the psychiatrist asked.

"I'm okay with them."

"Can you tell me again what you were feeling?"

"I was afraid," I said. "I was scared shitless when he pointed that pistol at me."

"Why did you feel you had no option except lethal force?"

"Because we kept yelling, *'Jesh! Jesh!'* He knew we were the Army and he could have surrendered at any time. When we first entered the room, he could have yelled something, but he didn't. He jumped out from behind the sofa with his gun. This kid didn't want us to take him alive."

"How do you know that?"

"I didn't kill him because I wanted to," I said. "I knew that if I didn't shoot him, then the other members of my team—Dedi, Yossi, Zoar—could've been shot. For me it was about keeping people alive who *wanted* to live. That's the one thing I'm certain of. When we came into that room, the kid clearly didn't want to live."

For the rest of the month, the only aspect of unit life I didn't participate in was going out on field missions. My training regimen became even more intense. What else could I do but invest my time polishing my skills, working on my Krav Maga, and shooting countless rounds on the firing ranges?

On the team, no one talked about fatal incidents with an eye toward soul-searching or hand-wringing. In wartime conditions, fatalities—on both sides—occur with grim regularity. And while there's hardly a commendation for killing a terrorist target or one of his accomplices during a mission, every soldier on the base knows he would have reacted in precisely the same fashion. We are *trained* to react with lightning reflexes in life-threatening situations. Veteran operators—especially the officers like Ilan and Zoar—had used lethal force on more than one occasion. No one talked about it this way, but a fatality like the one I was involved in was treated as a solemn rite of passage among my fellow warriors. It was a door most of us would have to pass through at some point and we all knew there was no going back. Killing a man changes you, but after the investigation wrapped up and I returned to active duty, I was even more mentally confident, more definitive in my actions, more clear about the need not to hesitate to use my weapon if I needed to protect the lives of my brothers.

TWENTY

Most warriors in the field start to isolate themselves at a certain point, disconnecting from everybody who's not a member of their team. After a few months of active missions, I found myself doing the same thing. I couldn't spend time socially with anyone outside the unit. Not even Golda.

During the year of my training, I used to like to ride my Suzuki over to the University of Tel Aviv and Hebrew University, to hang out with a couple of friends from Los Angeles who were on the Ulpan overseas program. I dated quite a few Jewish-American girls who, I'll be honest, tended to be impressed by an IDF uniform, especially on an American volunteer. But once I became operational, I was so disgusted by these spoiled, oblivious Americans, smoking hash and tripping on ecstasy on their cushy, protected campuses that I had to stop socializing with the students altogether.

On weekends off, I hung out exclusively with the team. We were a closed circle with Ilan as the nucleus. After a few months, Ilan and I ended up getting an apartment together in Givatayim, just outside Tel Aviv. It was a decent little flat where we could crash on our days off. It had two bedrooms, a microwave, and washing machine. We had a big TV that we never watched. Coming from barracks life, the biggest luxury was to have our own washing machine and dryer; we used to line up bags of fatigues, twelve complete uniforms each, and stand there running the machines nonstop for three straight days. While most of our crew headed home to their families in Tel Aviv while on leave, Ilan and I gassed up my Suzuki RF600 motorcycle and logged a lot of high-speed highway time together. We rode all over the Holy Land. We rode down through the desert to the Dead Sea, the lowest place on Earth, floated in the salty water as families of Bedouins came down to the banks to wash their laundry in the sea. Another weekend, we rode all the way to the port of Eilat without stopping—a brutal eight-hour haul to make on a motorcycle. We got to the beach and couldn't walk for three hours afterward.

Mostly, though, we covered the hills and farm country in the north. Even though he was half Sabra (through his Israeli-born father) and had spent years in Israel, Ilan knew very little about the kibbutznik experience. He'd gone straight into the IDF when he arrived and never got to mix it up with the American girls and the tourists the way I did. "You want to take a ride to my old kibbutz?" I suggested one morning.

I had told Ilan a lot of stories about the commandos I'd worked with at the fishpond, most of whom had been incredibly supportive, offering me advice on how to make it through the *gibush* and survive the brutal training months. But Gali, the high-ranking Matkalist, used to ridicule me constantly under his breath or bark orders in broken English. I used to spend a lot of Shabbat evenings at Dror Shapiro's house, where the fishpond guys hung out after work. Most of them still considered me an outsider—despite my working alongside them in the freezing water for weeks—but Gali considered me beneath contempt. He would stare at me hard, with palpable dislike: I wasn't Matkal, wasn't even a soldier, wasn't worth wasting his breath on.

When Ilan and I arrived at the kibbutz, we rode over to Dror's house—and who did we see right away? Gali. This was the first time I'd seen him since I'd passed through the grueling pipeline of the Special Forces. As I parked the bike, I could see him register the handgun and short-barreled M-16 I was wearing. I introduced Ilan to everyone.

To my complete shock, Gali greeted me in Hebrew. Before that day, he *never* spoke a word of Hebrew to me.

"Ah, there's a face I recognize," he said with a warm smile. "So how have you been?"

Gali looked me up and down approvingly, knowing exactly what I'd been through. He didn't say "congratulations," or "*Mazal tov!*" but being treated like a fellow warrior—and like a fellow Israeli—by a tough son of a bitch like Gali was as much a testament to the brotherhood of warriors I belonged to as earning that red beret after the *massa kumta*. And now that I'd been operational for several months, I even understood why Gali had treated me the way he had earlier.

At some point, you flip a psychological switch. *I will do whatever it takes to complete these missions, to do them safely, in a way that won't get me or my brothers killed.* You turn on an inner killer—a survival mechanism inherent in all of us but rarely used in normal, day-today Western society. After a month or two in the field, you can *never* turn it back off. It leaves you feeling angry, aggressive, and suspicious. No matter how easygoing and gregarious you were before you entered the unit, you never treat strangers, or even regular civilians, the same way again.

Standing there with Gali's hand on my shoulder, I realized that his cold behavior hadn't been because he disliked me or resented the fact that I was an American. He was simply looking through me. I might have been swimming in the fishpond two meters away, but to Gali I was invisible.

I now treated people the same way. In the back of my mind, whenever I met a stranger, I would think: *Do I know you? Why are you looking at me like I've met you? Did we go through* maslul *together?*

Yet I tried to avoid going to the extreme that Gali represented. On leave, whenever I passed another fighter in the street, even if he wasn't Special Forces, I knew he'd been through a tough year of combat training. I'd see his colored beret, and I'd always offer him a little nod of recognition.

When we got off the base the only things we wanted to do were sleep, drink, and fight. Ilan and I used to get bombed on Gold Star beer, and go hang out in the roughest pool halls and bars we could find in Tel Aviv. We weren't actively looking for trouble, but if a fight came our way, we certainly weren't about to walk away from it, especially in the *arsim* joints of south Tel Aviv. Down in the neighborhoods of Sh'chunat Hatikvah and Tel Kabir, and in cities like Bat Yam, there are all kinds of rough-edged hangouts, dominated by Sephardic tough guys who are clannish, suspicious, and always looking for a fight. There's an instantly recognizable look and dress code with the *arsim*—gold chains with the giant Magen David, body-hugging T-shirts and supertight jeans, slicked back hair, Nike Air Jordans fresh out of the box. A lot of macho posturing: "What the fuck are you looking at?" and "Hold me back, Dudu! Hold me back before I murder this fucking pussy!"

It would usually start with something as simple as Ilan asking a wannabe tough guy for a little more space to aim his pool cue. The guy would say, "Oh, excuse me," and then intentionally bump Ilan's arm with his hip so that he blew the shot. Before you knew it, the whole poolroom was a swarming brawl. We didn't give a shit about the numbers stacked against us; often we fought ten or twelve guys at a time. One of the *arsim* would pick up a pool stick and swing it at Ilan's head. Ilan would duck, pivot, and knock the guy out with one punch. I'd clock another guy in the head, then kick him in the chest. Bottles and glasses would start flying and we'd take off with a dozen cursing *arsim* chasing us out into street at two A.M.

And we didn't limit our aggression to bar fights. We constantly used our commando training to pull *zubut*. Duvdevan was infamous for the brutal and punishing nature of our practical jokes. While on leave, somebody from the unit was always getting his ass kidnapped, snatched off the street, thrown in the back of the car and punched, elbowed, and kicked before being dumped out into the street a few blocks away. They got me at least three times. You had to stay alert, prepared to fight off a snatch-and-grab at any time. I ended up with bruises and welts all over my body—no shots to the face were allowed—but I didn't care. We all came to consider the kidnapping *zubu* a gesture of love.

Ilan was the one fighter in the unit that no one could ever get.

Taking down Ilan would have been the king *zubu* of all time. He was too goddamn clever, paranoid, and aggressive to ever let his guard down. After a few months in the apartment with me, Ilan had moved out, buying a new apartment with his father, who was beginning to fly to Israel often on business from Australia. It was a brand-new condo in one of the most exclusive beachfront areas of Tel Aviv, and Ilan wasted no time installing three high-security Israeli deadbolts.

For months we'd been trying to get Ilan. Finally, we saw our chance when Ilan was physically smoked. He'd commanded eight missions in a row, running a series of intense ops in the territories. He'd been running and gunning for about eighty hours, and by the end of his triple shift, his eyes were at half-mast and we could see he was coasting on fumes.

We sent our teammate Moti, who'd borrowed all the professional equipment from his locksmith father, to make a mold of Ilan's locks. We had new keys made and broke into the apartment while Ilan was still out in the field. We knew that Ilan's father was flying in that night. We decided to redecorate the whole apartment, putting up Calvin Klein underwear ads, beefcake Speedo posters, nude models with hairy chests and Fu Manchu mustaches. Three of us hid just as Ilan's dad entered the new apartment. His jaw dropped, then he gasped. "What the fuck?" he said, and started ripping down all the pictures.

For almost an hour, he stormed around, slamming cupboard doors, until finally he went to bed. We remained hidden, completely silent. Around three in the morning Ilan opened the front door. Shrieking like banshees, we leapt out of our hiding places and kidnapped him, dragging him outside. When we got down to the street,

Dedi raced up in the getaway car. We threw Ilan in back, punching and elbowing him. Ilan's only about five eleven, 170 pounds, but he possesses a freakish strength. He was fighting us tooth and nail, kicking with everything he had. One of his punches caught me dead in the eye. It felt like he fractured my eye socket.

After a few blocks, we kicked Ilan's ass out of the car and left him to stagger home and explain to his father why the walls of their brand-new condominium were plastered with pictures of naked men.

Ilan was much more than my team leader and officer: he had become my mentor, best friend, as close as a blood brother. As the only two non–Israeli born guys in the unit, we had a special bond. I loved him but I had to admit—the blue-eyed Australian was out of his fucking head. Ilan was a fourth-degree black belt in Krav Maga, the best hand-to-hand commando in the unit, and he liked nothing better than walking around the base kicking raw unsuspecting first-year commandos as hard as he could in the gut.

Sometimes the glare in those pale eyes made him seem almost *too* professional, like a stainless-steel automaton programmed to kill on command.

He reminded me of a story my grandfather told me when I was a kid, the folktale of a rabbi in Prague who got sick of seeing the Jews in the ghetto terrorized and murdered and used powerful kabbalah to create a magical protector called the Golem. He sculpted it from clay, carved the word *emeth* (or "truth") in its forehead, and the clay man came to life. At first, the Jews were overjoyed; the Golem was a superhero at the ghetto gates, stopping all the anti-Semitic attacks.

But he also kept growing bigger, more violent, impossible to control, until the Jews were more terrified of the Golem than they'd been of the Christian persecutors.

It wasn't just Ilan—at times we all had a bit of the Golem in us. After three months of nonstop missions, a crack-up is inevitable. You've maxed out your circuitry. Your motherboard is fried. You've seen and done things that no shrink can help you with. So you deaden your senses with distractions—cigarettes, alcohol, and Russian party girls.

One weekend, Ilan, Nir, and I were on furlough, celebrating the takedown of a terrorist cell. We were wearing full beards, drunk out of our skulls, cruising around Tel Aviv in Ilan's bulletproof civilian car. A stray cat darted out into the street and we hit it—I heard the sickening sound of its body bouncing under our car. Ilan stopped the car, glanced in the rearview mirror, and saw the cat was still crawling. So he backed up and ran over it a second time. Again the cat's body thudded hideously as we passed over it. It wouldn't die. Ilan, laughing, took three more passes but still the cat was dragging its mangled body across the street.

I couldn't stand it. I jumped out of the car, whipped out my Sig Sauer P228, a 9-mm semiautomatic equipped with silencer, and fired three muted shots into the darkness. The cat's body was still. Ilan sat in the car laughing drunkenly, while Nir was pissing against a graffiti-covered wall.

I saw a seventy-year-old man in the shadows, stoop-shouldered, wearing a black fedora, his face creased with sadness. Our eyes locked. I felt my face flush with shame. *Who was I? What had I become?*

The old man saw our shaggy beards and my pistol and must have realized we weren't ordinary soldiers, but some type of undercover

Special Forces. As I opened the car door, he nodded at me, and gave me the kind of look you sometimes get from civilians in Israel: a silent acknowledgment that you're out there putting your balls on the line for the safety of the Israeli nation. Maybe my booze-addled brain just saw what it needed to see, but after putting the cat out of its misery, I took the old rabbi's nod as a gesture of absolution.

That drunken night in Tel Aviv, perhaps more than any other, helped me grasp why the commanding officers in Duvdevan determined that an operator can only be allowed to work on a team for a *maximum* of eight to ten months. The psychological stress of fieldwork can turn even the most balanced and emotionally grounded man into a wild-eyed Golem. After fifteen months of building and sharpening your Special Forces skills in training, a *mista'aravim* warrior's working stint in the territories is under a year, at which point he is physically and psychologically maxed out. The commanders need to begin the process of winding us down, taking what remains of our three years of military service to rotate us into a less stressful routine of advanced coursework at Mitkan Adam and employing us as instructors to train the new batch of recruits coming into the unit.

TWENTY-ONE

One morning in Tel Aviv as I was trying to sleep off a Gold Star hangover, my goddamned pager sounded. We were being called in for a Level Four meeting, meaning all the Duvdevan teams needed to be back at the base immediately. It would turn out to be the final major mission of my Spec Ops career.

Four hours later, the operation room was crowded, swirling with cigarette smoke. Zoar was sitting at the head of the table, next to Ilan, staring at the details of the terrorist warrant and breaking down the Ops plan.

"Tonight we've got a shot to take down Abu Jihad," he said. I glanced around the room—we all recognized the nom de guerre, meaning "father of the Holy War," of the Hamas mastermind behind the Dizengoff Mall bombing. "Shabak's been working this on the inside for months. We've seen several chances come and go. This guy moves around from safe house to safe house constantly. We understand Abu Jihad's going to be at a wedding, just outside of Nablus. We're going to insert a small team undercover in the wedding party. We'll take him down right after the ceremony, at the reception hall."

I would be working *mista'aravim*, but I wouldn't be going inside the wedding reception. I was going to pose as a Palestinian sweet-corn vendor, acting as one of the eyes-on-target. The mission was so high-priority that Command had requested multiple and simultaneous eyes-on-target confirmations.

It was a huge operation, probably the most complex and well planned of my time with Duvdevan. Close to forty warriors worked on the mission, divided into four teams. Twenty men were going in undercover, two inside the wedding reception hall, posing as friends of the groom, and the rest walking around outside to confirm the target's arrival. Rooftop snipers surrounded the target location. We had a dozen undercover cars with heavy weaponry on the perimeter, circling the streets of Nablus.

We spent hours in the operations room, going over the logistics. We had guys on the inside who'd been to the target locations a few days earlier; they'd taken photos of the area, mapping the streets. We even had the floor plan of the community hall where the party was going to be held. We knew which door Abu Jihad was most likely to enter. The most unpredictable element was the street outside. Streams of people would be coming in and out constantly, cars would be double-parked, blocking our lines of vision and possible escape routes.

It was a tight-knit neighborhood, staunchly loyal to Hamas, virtually impossible to infiltrate for any long period of time. The informal and unstructured nature of the wedding reception—more of a communal celebration for the neighborhood than a formal gathering with place cards and an RSVP list—gave us our window of opportunity. This section of Nablus was such a hotbed of Hamas leadership and recruitment that they felt completely secure. Who would have the audacity to try to crash this wedding party?

By seven P.M. I approached the wedding hall, wearing a thin-striped dress shirt, dark gray slacks, and a fake mustache attached with mustard glue, pushing my sweet-corn cart down the block. Our undercover guys would have about sixty seconds to walk inside, shake some hands, offer congratulations, and then snatch Abu Jihad.

My primary role as one of the eyes-on-target would be to confirm that Abu Jihad had actually shown up at the reception. We had to make certain that it was him, not some look-alike double or cousin with a close resemblance. We had a series of surveillance photos, taken with extremely high-powered long-lens cameras and enlarged into razor-sharp close-ups. Back at the base, I had studied the photographs for hours, and I knew Abu Jihad's distinguishing features, right down to the mole above one eyebrow.

I wheeled my vending cart into position, with a clear line of sight on the entrance to the reception hall. My undercover disguise was not designed to withstand deep scrutiny. The reason playing a sweet-corn vendor was a good role was that the actual vendors changed a lot, providing one of the few excuses for new faces in the neighborhood. For the same reason, we also had several undercover operators driving taxis because there were lots of unofficial gypsy cabs in the territories.

I saw one of the passing cabs. The driver was a Duvdevan operator, and the passengers in back were also our operators. For the next fifteen minutes, our cabdrivers dropped off their passengers and picked up new passengers, adding another layer of eyes on the target as they circled the neighborhood.

My cart had a handwritten sign in Arabic listing my prices: sweet corn for one dinar each. The cart also had a live-action camera feed, meaning I had to position it carefully to capture images of the front entrance. If a firefight were to break out, I had my Sig P228 tucked at the small of my back and the bottom of the cart was custom-lined with Kevlar. Flipped on its side, it would provide cover as a bulletproof barricade.

"Salaam."

I looked up to see a guy about my age handing me a dinar coin. I handed him one ear of corn. I didn't want to risk making conversation, so I looked away. Luckily, it was the only sale I made during the mission.

My earbud was in place. As soon as we had confirmation that Abu Jihad was on the scene, my instructions were to double-click. I could hear transmissions from one of the circling white Savannahs in which the officers were receiving camera feed from my sweet-corn cart as well as other video images coming from several undercovers carrying briefcases and backpacks with cameras.

Every one of the eyes-on-target—there were more than a dozen in the immediate vicinity—was instructed to double-click upon confirmation of sighting Abu Jihad so there would be no chance of false identification. Zoar and Ilan were adamant: We needed double-clicks from everyone working eyes-on-target before initiating the takedown. If any of us decided to call it off, we each had a squelch button that would transmit a high-pitched tone to everyone on the team, letting them know that the mission had been aborted.

My team was designated as the second cordon. The first cordon was responsible for the security of the two operators entering the reception hall as wedding guests. The second cordon was responsible for the takedown vehicles—SUVs from the Duvdevan base to be used when Abu Jihad and any accomplices were apprehended—while the third cordon, still about a kilometer out, consisted of bulletproof green IDF vehicles equipped with heavy machine guns for use in the event of a riot or massive neighborhood shoot-out.

An older model Mercedes sedan pulled up in front of the reception hall, double-parking. Three men exited, all wearing open-necked dress shirts. All were in their late twenties or early thirties, dark-complexioned with mustaches and trimmed beards. As they approached the entrance to the reception hall, I recognized the face of Abu Jihad. I gave the double-click.

Zoar's voice came on my earbud, shouting.

"Are you sure? Is everyone sure?"

One by one, all the other eyes-on-target double-clicked.

If anyone clicked a third time, or if Abu Jihad got spooked and started to run, we had orders to break cover, transition immediately from *mista'aravim* into takedown mode.

The two officers assigned to infiltrate the wedding were legends in the unit, with hundreds of missions under their belts. Seasoned and cool-headed, they didn't hesitate, and they didn't panic.

They walked directly into the reception hall and we could hear the casual exchanges as they shook a few hands, offering congratulations, saying, *"Salaam aleikum."*

Boom—it all transpired within six seconds.

The two operators grabbed Abu Jihad, without drawing their weapons, and pulled him outside the wedding hall by his elbows and shoulders. He was struggling, his face a mask of confusion, but he barely had time to shout. The moment our operators yanked him outside, an unlicensed taxi with three more of our operators inside lurched to a screeching stop. The back door flew open. Abu Jihad was bundled inside. The taxi made a clean getaway.

It was all over so fast that everyone inside the hall was stunned. Abu Jihad had no formal bodyguards, but one of the wedding guests now rushed outside, enraged, drawing a pistol from his waistband. He brandished the black handgun. But before he could get off a shot there was the crack of rifle fire. Three whistling reports. He fell to the pavement dead.

Three of our rooftop snipers hit him with nearly simultaneous telescopic shots. The wedding guests were streaming out into the street, shouting, pointing.

"Allāhu Akbar! Allāhu Akbar!"

It was a scene of pure mayhem. People were shrieking; women were falling to the ground; and still no one knew which direction the gunshots came from, how Abu Jihad was kidnapped from the reception so quickly, how this other guest ended up bleeding to death in the street.

I reached behind me and felt for my Sig on the small of my back. But there was no need to pull it now. The mission was completed. I could see the taillights of the getaway taxi carrying Abu Jihad rounding the corner. As casually as possible, I ditched my sweet-corn cart, walking off in the direction of the predetermined rendezvous spot a block away.

When I got there, another undercover taxi was pulling over to the curb.

Ilan was at the wheel, smoking a cigarette, radio in his lap. Inon was in the backseat, grabbing me by the elbow as I opened the door, pulling me inside the moving cab.

Now Ilan's radio began to crackle with more fast-breaking news. Two other wanted Hamas terrorists were spotted as guests inside the reception hall.

There was no more element of surprise. Duvdevan's job was done. The order was given for the third cordon to go to work. The uniformed brigades from Golani and Givati were ordered to snatch up the other two wanted men.

The stealth *mista'aravim* mission was over; it had now turned into a massive display of military might. As Ilan wheeled the undercover taxi around the corner, I watched the scene unfolding outside my window: over a hundred IDF soldiers taking up positions; the bulletproof armored vehicles beginning to roll, surrounding the reception hall. As I was leaving Nablus, the entire neighborhood looked like it was under siege.

PART IV

TWENTY-TWO

By the last few months of my tour, I was trying to spend as much time away from the base as possible. I would jump on my motorcycle, bouncing up north to the kibbutz, or down to Eilat, or into Tel Aviv to hang out at the beach. I was doing all kinds of extracurricular training like going back to Wingate for two weeks for some ridiculous master's fitness course. I was doing anything I could to take my mind off the desensitizing brutality of the missions.

By the end of my rotation—and this is true for every soldier I ever met—I found myself literally counting down the days until my army service ended. It was like those old black-and-white prison movies where the convicts scratch lines in the cell wall. My contract was for two years and eleven months, and in the final weeks, I was taking a pen and marking off the days on my calendar.

Although I was still permanently attached to a team during my final three months in Duvdevan, my assignment was like being in a bullpen, remaining on call, prepping younger soldiers who were advancing through the pipeline.

Since I didn't have to remain on base, and I already had all the requisite gun permits and security certificates, I signed up to work as a security guard at my old kibbutz during this deceleration period. I patrolled the grounds at night and manned the front gate armed with an Uzi. It was the first inkling I had that my advanced military skills could be put to use doing some form of security work. I spent long weekends on the kibbutz and at the homes of the former commandos, having Shabbat dinners, singing and talking over wine with Dror, Uri, and their wives, detaching myself from the pace and rigors of army life.

I'd never truly experienced Israel as anything other than a kibbutz worker or a soldier. I used my days off during this period to travel around as a tourist. In terms of pure geography—let alone archaeology—Israel is one of the most spectacular places on earth. From the vineyards of the Golan Heights to the waterfall oasis of Ein Gedi on the shore of the Dead Sea (where the Bible says David hid from King Saul three thousand years ago), I covered the entire country. I rode out to Masada, where the zealots had chosen collective suicide over being conquered by the Roman army. I went to the *Kotel*—the Western retaining wall of the Temple Mount—which for centuries has been the most sacred place on earth to the Jewish people, and tucked a small Hebrew prayer into a crack in one of the massive blocks of stone. In the north, I visited Beit Shearim, a series of caves containing two-thousand-year-old limestone and marble sarcophagi decorated with menorahs and other Judaic symbols. Visiting those archaeological wonders helped give me a better perspective not just on Israel's history but on my own IDF career, the dangerous missions I'd undertaken to protect this land which—despite the anti-Zionist propaganda—has had an unbroken Jewish presence for thousands of years.

After getting the tourist bug out of my system, I went back to Mitkan Adam for an entire month, teaching basic training and advanced instruction with handguns. Inon, one of my closest friends on the team, had been given the huge responsibility of overseeing all the new recruits for their seven months of basic and advanced training. Inon was always the natural star in the unit, and now he was being singled out for his leadership potential. He was on track toward officers' school—he ultimately did become a very high ranking officer—and being charged with bringing along an entire class of new recruits is one of the first big tests for the next generation of leaders.

As soon as Inon took the assignment he asked me to accompany him to Adam. He knew I was restless and searching for what would come next for me.

"Come on, Aaron," he said. "Just come with me. It'll be fun."

I taught basic marksmanship to the recruits. They were young Israelis, most of whom had just turned eighteen, starting at square one in the training program. I was only two years older than most of them, but they seemed like children to me. I kept muttering to myself, *Holy shit, these guys look like babies.*

As an instructor at Adam you're expected to be an asshole, to kick the shit out of the new guys to let them know where they are now—this isn't some regular tank unit, the infantry or the paratroopers. I knew the role I was supposed to assume, but I couldn't do it. I didn't have it in me to be as deranged and sadistic to the new kids as our instructors had been to us. I remembered how dispiriting the whole process could be. All too often, when I should have been screaming and ordering them to do punishment push-ups, I would find myself taking pity on the exhausted-looking recruits and opt for a softer approach.

One day on the rifle range, I noticed an eighteen-year-old trainee who looked hopelessly lost and confused. In his eyes I saw that he was *zayin nishbar*—his dick was broken. I took the kid aside and whispered to him.

"Are you okay, man? You better get your shit together now. Clear the cobwebs and find your mental focus. If you don't, you're toast. You have no idea what's about to happen to you from this point forward."

I was in the middle of instructing the trainees in shooting when Ilan came to tell me that we were invited to a weekend get-together at Colonel Muki's house. For a first lieutenant like Ilan this wasn't so unusual, but for a regular soldier like me, to receive an invitation to the C.O.'s house was a very big deal. As we got on my Suzuki, Ilan also implied that Muki wanted to talk to me about extending my military service, about my taking the examinations for officers' school.

Like a lot of senior officers, Colonel Muki had a big farm up in Zichron Yaakov, not far from my old kibbutz. When Ilan and I pulled my bike up the driveway, we saw a few of the fighters from the fishpond, guys from Matkal and S-13, sitting around, smoking Marlboros, drinking Gold Stars. Everyone was in jeans, T-shirts, and

Oakleys, completely casual, enjoying the sunset and warm breeze. There was a volleyball game in one corner of the yard.

A lot of high-ranking officers were at the party, even a few generals. The Weiss brothers weren't there, but their father was milling about, small glass of whiskey in hand. Their dad was a full colonel, a famous ex-commando from S-13 whom I'd never met, but I'd heard the stories. He was old-school and he'd been Muki's commanding officer when Muki was coming up through S-13. The elder Weiss was a tall strapping guy with gray hair, walking around without shoes or sandals. He had the classic kibbutznik look, exuding toughness, with deeply tanned and leathery skin; the soles of his feet were giant calluses from walking barefoot all the time. He offered me one of his rough, powerful hands in greeting.

"Oh, Aaron! My sons told me about you."

He gestured down the path, where Colonel Muki was tending to one of his tomato vines.

"Go catch Muki while the sonuvabitch is gardening. I think he wants to talk to you about something."

I'd had conversations with Muki a few times on the base, but never a normal one-to-one talk. In our unit, the rank-and-file didn't have too many opportunities to socialize with the commanding officer. All Muki knew about me was that I was Ilan's American protégé, the blue-eyed Australian's up-and-coming understudy from Beverly Hills.

"Ma ha-inyanim?" Muki asked as I approached.

"Beseder."

"I wanted to speak to you about something." The whole time he was talking to me, Muki didn't stop scrutinizing his goddamn tomatoes. "Look, I don't know if you're interested—it'll be a big commitment in terms of time and energy—but I want you to give it some serious thought, okay?"

Muki never actually said the words "officers' school," but I knew what he meant. In fact, he danced around the subject in a distracted way, stooping down, picking at withered leaves, working his beloved tomato patch.

"Aaron," he said finally, with a little grunt. "How much time do you have?"

"I'm in my last month, sir."

"So what are you thinking about after all this?"

"I'm thinking—honestly, sir, I'm thinking, 'Beverly Hills.'"

The colonel pulled a few dead leaves off one of his tomato vines and crumpled them into this fist. Then he laughed softly. "You know what?" he said. "I'd be thinking the same thing if I were you."

I had never given much thought to pursuing officers' school. Ilan was natural officer material; Inon, too. But *me*? Two things weighed heavily in making my decision. First, there was an insanely tough entrance exam. Ilan had flunked the officers' exam several times before he finally passed. My oral Hebrew was good enough, but my written skills weren't. To be honest, I didn't have a prayer of passing the entrance exam.

Second, I would have had to sign up for another year and a half of service. At this point, my dick was *beyond* broken. I couldn't wait to get out of the army. The mystique and the sense of wonder about Duvdevan had worn off long ago. I felt like I'd pulled back the curtain and seen Oz. Even if by some miracle I had passed the written officer's exam, I knew in my bones that a lifelong military career wasn't for me. In part, the fatigue of living like a filthy flea-infested dog for so many years had taken its toll. For all the financial resources that go into training each commando, the Israeli military has bare-bones living facilities.

But beyond personal comfort I'd started to see a more profound rationale behind the mandatory three-year limit for general draftees and volunteers. After nearly thirty-six months of hard-core training and undercover work, something deeper than exhaustion sets in: you start venturing into a dark, scary zone in the human psyche. No matter how much you believe in the justness of the mission, it takes a special type of personality—an intense level of commitment I'd seen in men like Zoar and Ilan—to function long-term as a professional warrior.

The career of an undercover commando is a furious meteor's flash. There's a phrase I often heard muttered by IDF infantrymen and Border Patrol grunts when we'd cross paths. The *real* warriors, they'd say, storm into the room with *retzach b'enayim*—"murder in the eyes." At first I took it as a compliment, an acknowledgment that we were the hardened warriors unfazed by bloodshed, who wouldn't hesitate with our fingers on the trigger. We were the guys you want storming into a terrorist hideout if your mother or sister is taken hostage. But as I hit the end of my tour, I began to see that *retzach b'enayim* label in a far different light.

Alone in the three A.M. darkness of the barracks, I'd lie awake tallying up the near-misses and catastrophes of my missions. How many times could I keep rolling the dice before my number came up? How many times could I come *this* close to blowing the brains out of some twelve-year-old Palestinian schoolgirl whose only crime was living in a house with her terrorist father? How many missions could I complete before I watched one of my best friends get blown away? Every day was another game of Russian roulette. It was only a matter of time—the hourglass measuring weeks rather than years—before my mother back in L.A. got that intercontinental phone call: *We regret to inform you that last night your son made the ultimate sacrifice for the State of Israel.* Another solemn barracks sitting *shivah*; another framed photograph to be saluted and toasted with warm vodka even as the cold cadaver is autopsied in a military morgue; another Jewish mother asking, "Why didn't you protect my son?"

The thing I hadn't considered before turning down officer school was how negatively my decision could affect Ilan's career. It was a huge insult to him and it had major repercussions up the chain of command. I can be a self-centered asshole sometimes—I have to admit—and back then, I only saw it from my perspective. I was exhausted, burned out, and ready to leave army life behind. But Ilan had gone out on a limb, convincing his superior officers to give me a shot at the prestigious, highly competitive school. Even though the unit commander knew me and what I was capable of doing in an operational situation, the mere fact of my being an American made me a very unlikely candidate. But Ilan had vouched for me, sworn that I had what it took to lead men in the field.

We didn't have a verbal falling-out, partly because I hadn't even thought to tell Ilan to his face that I'd rejected Colonel Muki's offer. He just heard about it through the unit grapevine. After that, Ilan's demeanor turned quiet and passive-aggressive. He never confronted me about the issue, but he would shoot me these sidelong glances and make a hundred cutting remarks. I knew he'd stuck his neck out for me, made some recommendations, and I'd turned the offer down. *Big fucking deal!* I said to myself. But, as I was later to learn once I'd returned to the States, it was a big fucking deal to Ilan.

The process for leaving the army was surprisingly easy. The first step was to report to my original Bakum, the induction center, just outside Tel Aviv. Every soldier is required to turn in all the clothing he was originally issued—two pairs of pants, T-shirts, standard-issue army boots, socks, and underwear. The joke within the IDF is that no one can ever find the original articles of clothing after three years of service so everyone spends that last day or two scrounging around the barracks, borrowing other guys' stuff to turn in and satisfy the sergeant at the Bakum with his clipboard checklist. After turning in your uniform, the sergeant gives you a computerized printout indicating that you've been formally discharged from the army. Then I had to make one last trip through the territories to the Duvdevan base, where I turned in all my expensive gear: bulletproof vests, helmets, night-vision goggles, and short-barreled M-16 and several handguns.

I realized that the only way to leave Israel was to do it quickly. I booked a nonrefundable one-way ticket. I packed up my apartment in Tel Aviv, sold off my television and my furniture. As soon as I booked the flight, I called my mother to say: "It's done. I'm out. I'll be back in a few weeks."

Ilan and Inon helped me pack up my remaining belongings. What I didn't sell or pack, I simply ditched. I had to wait around until I got my final deposit back on the apartment from my landlord. Then Ilan drove me to the hotel where I was staying for my last few nights.

My last morning in Israel, we said our good-byes in the hotel lobby, just before I hopped in a cab for the airport. We kept everything short and sweet. Ilan shot me one of his frightening pale-eyed stares, looking like he was getting ready to punch me in the jaw. Then he gave me a hug, turned, and walked away. He was never one for lingering or reminiscing.

TWENTY-THREE

When I came back to Los Angeles that summer, I did nothing but sleep for weeks. I'd wake up, force myself to eat something, and then just crawl back to bed. I didn't want to face the world.

I should have gone to see a shrink. I couldn't answer the most fundamental question: *What the fuck am I supposed to do when I get out of bed?* During my army years, I knew exactly what I was supposed to wear, what I was supposed to eat, where I supposed to be nearly every single moment of every day. Now I was suddenly in charge of my own affairs. I felt a crushing vacuum around me, like I couldn't breathe.

I didn't know what the hell to do with my time. It's different for the average Israeli soldier who can generally go back to a supportive home environment where everyone—his father, mother, brothers and sisters, even his grandparents—has shared the military experience. Many young Israelis today finish their three years of army service and travel the world for a year. Throw on a backpack and head off to Europe, the Himalayas, New Zealand, Bali. It's a smart way to cope with the empty and disorienting feeling of leaving the army.

I was back in Beverly Hills, only twenty-one years old, but I had the real-world experience of a man twice my age. I was either sullen and silent all day long, or my mother and I would be fighting tooth and nail, screaming at each other until we were both hoarse.

I couldn't get along with anyone else, either. I experienced radical mood swings. I had so much aggression bottled up inside me that I would snap at any provocation. I couldn't go to a bar without getting into a fistfight. Someone would start talking shit to me, I'd pounce, throw a few punches to the head, then walk out to my car and drive off before the cops showed up.

I'd be sitting in a Hollywood bar, some girl telling me that she wanted to be a famous actress *so* bad—*so* bad—and I was thinking, *Do you have any idea what's going on right now on the other side of the world?*

Or I'd run into one of my buddies from high school who was working in the film industry.

"Dude! How was Israel? How was the army?"

How could I even begin to answer those questions? How could I explain what it was like to dress up as an Arab and drive through the streets of Jenin at two A.M. on the hunt for a known mass murderer, what it felt like to kill a terrorist in a gunfight or to cradle a dying teenager in my arms? These weren't experiences any of my old friends from high school could begin to grasp, so I didn't bother trying to explain. I would simply shrug and walk away.

I was so conflicted and confused that I started regretting not staying in the army and going to officer school. I felt like an abject failure. I remembered a guy named Ze'ev who'd shown up on the kibbutz for a few weeks when I was working in the fishponds. The first time I laid eyes on Ze'ev, I could tell that he was totally fucked up. He would come down to the edge of the fishpond, talking to himself like a schizophrenic.

"What's the deal with him?" I asked Dror while we were wading together in the freezing water.

"Ze'ev? Oh, he was *mista'aravim.*"

The story was that Ze'ev had been hit in the head with a rock during an undercover mission in the territories and was in the hospital for weeks. He nearly died and was permanently pulled out of operational status because of his injury. In the kibbutz cafeteria, I tried to talk to him a few times but Ze'ev would stare back at me, not answering my questions, then walk away.

Ze'ev was actually the first *Duvdevanist* I'd ever met, months before my first encounter with Ilan at Wingate. He was mentally *gone,* too far gone to even work competently at the fishponds. Looking back, I realized it wasn't a rock to the head that had done the damage. Ze'ev had run too many missions and they'd left him in a state of perpetual rage, depression, and isolation.

I never got as bad as Ze'ev, but I was clinically depressed once I got home, yet too proud to acknowledge there was something wrong with me. Eventually, the depression got me in a chokehold and I could hardly communicate. Los Angeles seemed like the shallowest place on earth, the people full of their own sense of importance and entitlement. Even my parents. I used to watch them working on their projects, printing out their screenplays or going off to their lunch meetings, and I'd ask myself: "What the hell do you people *do* for a living? What's the *point* of any of this? Who do you think it matters to?"

At night, I'd drive around in a total daze. The celebrity restaurants, the flocks of paparazzi swarming around red-carpet premieres; L.A. became the most absurd and illogical city on earth, a metropolis built around making entertainment for the richest, most spoiled country on the planet. Whole days went by when I didn't open my mouth. There's a sarcastic expression in Hebrew that means, essentially, "Never mind wasting my words, I'm not even going to bother *opening* my mouth for you."

I was so filled with contempt and disillusionment that I couldn't even get a job. I lived on what was left of my bar mitzvah money and the pittance I'd earned in the IDF (1,500 shekels, or $350 a month). I was drinking too much, hanging out in bars, never talking about Israel. Never talking about the army. I was a clam.

When my savings were gone, I started doing all kinds of dead-end jobs, telemarketing, bouncing, bartending—short-term gigs I would find in the classified section of the *Los Angeles Times*. I was in a dangerous downward spiral until I woke up one morning, looked in the mirror, and realized I needed to get the hell out of L.A.

I booked a flight to Canada to visit Colonel Bowman at the Robert Land Academy. My original plan was to visit Bowman for a day or two. But he could see I was in rough shape emotionally. Once again, he took me under his wing. He never said anything directly but I knew that he was proud of my Special Forces service in the IDF—this was the guy, after all, who had sparked my imagination with those shiny Israeli jump wings on his lapel and his stories about the courage, devotion, and cunning of the Israeli military.

"Look, Aaron, whatever you need, you've got it," he said. "I'll give you any job you want."

Obviously, I couldn't teach—I didn't have the credentials—but Colonel Bowman created a special position for me. I did some odds and ends in the office part time, but primarily I was a drill instructor, training the students in basic military techniques on the parade grounds. At first, I thought my sojourn would last for a week or two. But I liked being back at the academy so much that I ended up renting a little apartment in town and staying for more than six months.

Most of the teachers at the school were former Canadian soldiers who'd seemed so scary and hard-core when I was a kid. Now they looked like a bunch of puffed-up Dudley Do-Rights who'd never really seen a life-and-death combat situation. It was like going back to a playground you remembered from childhood, where the stairs to the slide seemed to reach into the clouds, and realizing the thing was only five feet off the ground.

A lot of the instructors would wear their Canadian army insignia on their school uniforms. To me, that seemed pretentious. I had my IDF jump wings, my Duvdevan insignia, and my badge from the Counter Terror School, but I never wore any of them. The students knew I was some ex-boy from ten years back, that I'd done something-or-other in the Israeli army. But I never told them what I'd been trained in. Colonel Bowman never asked me about the kinds of missions I'd done, and, at the time, I wasn't ready to talk to anyone about my experiences.

I still had a lot of rage bottled up inside me, and the Canadian winters—short days, lack of sunlight, the added stress of being on an isolated school campus—brought out the worst in me. One night I went out drinking. I was alone, but just like in the old days with Ilan, I got trashed, drinking beer and playing pool in some dive. I wound up in an altercation with some hulking hockey player from the town. I don't remember exactly how it started, but suddenly his pool cue came swinging at me like a scythe. I blocked the stick, took it away from him, and proceeded to give him a bad beating. I lumped him up enough that the cops were called, and although I was lucky enough not to get arrested, stories were circulating around the school the next morning that I had pulled some Israeli Special Forces "trained-killer shit" at the local watering hole.

I ended up missing the next day of work and the new headmaster—Bowman being semiretired and acting as the chairman of the board—wanted to boot my ass out. But Bowman stepped up and said, "Don't even think about it. The kid isn't going anywhere. He can stay here as long as he wants."

After I'd slept off my hangover, a new realization hit me like a gut punch: I missed the *hell* out of Ilan. He'd been my closest companion, my roommate, my barroom brawling buddy for years; more important, we'd worked shoulder-to-shoulder in some of the most dangerous terrain in the West Bank—and then, practically overnight, the plug was pulled on our friendship. We hadn't spoken since I'd left Israel and, over the months, I felt like our rift had deepened. That day, I called the Duvdevan base and, to my total surprise, learned that Ilan wasn't with the unit anymore. The secretary who answered told me Ilan was gone, but she wasn't allowed to divulge the details of when he left or where he was now, typically secretive Army bullshit. I was at a total loss. I didn't have any contact numbers for him in Australia, but I started digging around on the Internet, tracking down any family connection I could find. After about a week, I got his mother on the phone, and she gave me Ilan's number. The phone rang about five times before he answered.

"Ilan!" I shouted. "Where the fuck are you, dude?"

"You're calling me, idiot. I'm in Melbourne."

"I *know*, but what are you doing in Melbourne?"

"I quit the unit."

"What do you mean you quit?"

"The new unit commander came in and he fucked with me. I told him to fuck off and I quit. End of story."

The new unit commander had come in from S-13 with a reputation for running a tight ship. Ilan was in charge of all the C.T. training for the unit. "The new C.O. thinks his shit don't stink, starts to question how I was running the C.T. program," Ilan told me. "So I put in my fuckin' papers the next morning."

Just like that he was out of the Army. But I knew that wasn't the *whole* story. The rift with the new C.O. was just the straw that broke the camel's back. My leaving had changed everything for him. Ilan had been my rock throughout those Duvdevan years, and I'd become his rock, too. I'd been feeling guilty for months.

"So when are you coming to Australia?" he asked.

I said I was teaching up at my old military school near Toronto, and I was just getting back on my feet. Frankly, I told him, I didn't have the money to travel to Australia, but somehow I knew we'd see each other again soon.

When I hung up I felt like I'd just dropped one of those punishment weight-belts the instructors at Robert Land used to make us wear when running laps. It was such a relief talking to Ilan again. It helped me get a grip.

I managed to finish up the rest of the semester without another incident like the bar fight. During that time, my friendship with Colonel Bowman also deepened. There was a deep current of respect and mutual understanding that flowed both ways. He knew I'd done something extraordinary, something I wasn't ready to share with him, and he left me alone. Much like he had done ten years before, he nurtured me, gave me a home and helped me regain my equilibrium until we both realized I was finally ready to make a life for myself back in California.

TWENTY-FOUR

I returned to L.A. and got my own apartment. Back when I was doing various odd jobs, answering classified ads in the *Los Angeles Times,* I'd taken a short-term security gig where I found myself working alongside a couple of regular infantry IDF veterans who'd found employment doing bodyguard work. Returning from Robert Land, a lightbulb went off and I started digging around the Israeli ex-pat community in Southern California. It wasn't long before I located a small group of ex-Israeli soldiers working for one particular security company.

I whipped together a résumé. The company called me two weeks later. Before I knew it, I was getting calls from six different companies, places where I'd never even sent my résumé, because word started to spread like a computer virus: "There's an Israeli Special Forces kid who is actually *legal* to work here." Since most of the guys who came to California from Israel weren't naturalized Americans and didn't have green cards, I was a hot commodity on the private-security circuit in L.A.

The first company I worked for specialized in celebrity security. And the first contract they gave me was guarding Brad Pitt's house. I went from being unemployed one day to being one of the lead security agents charged with running a major twenty-four-hour detail. Pitt had a stalker at the time. I organized the shifts, selected the security staff, and ended up working his house for about a year and a half.

As I did more celebrity bodyguarding around town, it became obvious that I could provide a higher quality of service if I ran my own company and implemented as many techniques from my IDF days as possible. I also realized that I could contribute something far more relevant than red-carpet muscle. I could serve an untapped market in the United States by offering counterterrorism skills and expertise that few Americans—even those in law enforcement and the military—had access to. So in the fall of 2000, I filed my incorporation papers as IMS Security. This was a full year before 9/11 but the blood-red scrawl was already on the wall: the 1993 World Trade Center attack; the truck bombings of the Khobar Towers in Saudi Arabia and the U.S. embassies in Kenya and Tanzania; the Al Qaeda attack on the destroyer U.S.S. *Cole* as it lay anchored off the coast of Yemen.

I decided I would staff my company exclusively with ex-Israeli Special Forces. The first guy I hired was Dedi. He moved to L.A., got his papers straight, and helped me build the company from the ground up, training new employees and constantly looking for new clients. (Dedi lives in the San Fernando Valley now, and directs much of our day-to-day operations. One of the great pleasures of my life is working alongside ex-fighters like Dedi.)

Our reputation spread fast, and we started signing up several big-ticket accounts, doing celebrity protection for A-list stars such as Jackie Chan and Arnold Schwarzenegger. However, our overwhelming focus was fast becoming the counterterrorism aspect of our business: firearms training, vehicle assault-takedowns and entry techniques, and hostage-crisis management. I hadn't thought of training members of law enforcement, until my crew was working a red-carpet premiere one night, and several LAPD noticed the low-key yet military-style operation Dedi and I were running. It was clear to them at a glance that we weren't run-of-the-mill Hollywood bodyguards.

One of the cops called me over. "Do you guys do training?" he asked.

Even though I had no idea what the LAPD was currently trained in, or how I would design and structure a course for civilian police based on an Israeli counterterrorism model, I instinctively agreed.

"Of course," I said. "We do law-enforcement training."

My first seminar didn't go well. I was raw and green and I tried to pack too much information into one course. I didn't realize how little the LAPD had been taught about the science of counterterrorism. And to be honest, pre-9/11, the type of Israeli Special Forces training I was offering was too hard-core to be palatable in the American marketplace. For example, an American police academy will typically train its officers to neutralize an "active shooter"—a gun-wielding perpetrator who has already killed or is clearly intent on killing—by firing two shots to the body and one to the head. That's it. Three shots and then they're supposed to assess the situation. Honestly, most cops I've trained are so frightened of the post-shooting peer review, the reams of paperwork, and the ironclad justifications they'll have to provide to their superiors for having discharged their weapon in the line of duty that it prevents them from being effective in the street. This restrictive, bureaucratic approach to using lethal force would be seen as laughably ineffective to anyone who'd passed through the rigorous courses at Mitkan Adam's Counter-Terror School.

Meanwhile, I had a secret fantasy that Ilan would move to California and become my partner in the business. He kept busting my balls to come to Australia, but at first I was too broke, then the business started to take off and I was too busy to think about traveling. We hadn't had another heart-to-heart talk on the phone since I had called from Canada. And then one night he showed up in Beverly Hills.

He had tracked down my mother's unlisted number, shown up at her house, introduced himself, and convinced my mother to give him her car keys so he could go find me.

I was sitting at an outdoor table at the Coffee Bean on Beverly Drive when Ilan pulled up in my mother's BMW, jumped out of the car, and proceeded to create a huge scene, wrestling me to the ground and throwing some serious punches and Krav Maga strikes. We must have fought in the street for a full minute before we both doubled over in laughter, hugging each other for the longest time.

We went out and we buried the hatchet completely. We didn't talk about the guilt, the bad feelings, about me leaving the Army the way I did—we just put it past us. We'd been shot at together in Jenin, Ramallah, gone undercover deep in the rock-throwing chaos of the territories. Did we think we were going to hold a *grudge* over something so trivial?

We stayed drunk for three days straight. We didn't talk about anything of substance, just threw back shots of whiskey and beer and had the best weekend I've ever had in my life.

Then on September 11, the whole world changed. When I watched those terrified people jumping from the uppermost floors of the World Trade Center, I was gutted. That moment hammered home the vast information gulf between the Israeli and American societies. The United States may have built the most awesome, technologically sophisticated military machine in human history, but the superpower's underbelly was soft and unprepared. We needed a massive paradigm shift in the way we thought about security—but how many Americans, I wondered, were prepared for the new world order? Almost immediately, my phone started ringing with requests from law enforcement.

Israeli-style tactics are the only proven method to successfully deal with terrorists on a tactical level. There's no fail-safe way to prevent terror attacks, but of all the countries in the world, Israel has come as close as possible to perfecting the methodology. And, I quickly realized, very few people in America knew as much as I did about that methodology.

IMS is a lean company, just twenty-three guys on staff. I don't want to be the biggest security and risk-assessment company in the market, employing five thousand guards who work at shopping malls and office complexes. All my staff have Special Forces backgrounds, either Duvdevan, Matkal, S-13, or Yamam, the civilian police counterterrorism unit. Today, within the Israeli Special Forces community, almost everybody knows about my company. In fact there's a flyer posted in the cafeteria on the Duvdevan base. If you can get U.S. work papers, you call Aaron Cohen.

Our training courses for American law enforcement are extremely technical. It's an uphill battle, even getting them to rethink the way they employ their handguns. For example, American military and police personnel learn a standardized way to aim and shoot. In Israel, though it may sound counterintuitive, the technique of pointing and shooting *without aiming* becomes second nature. When you're under pressure, your body tends to react by tightening; the time it takes you to consciously aim can put everything in the operation at risk. The Israeli technique allows you, in one fluid motion, to assume a stable shooting platform, firing with twice the accuracy in a shorter period of time. This is all part of the Israeli C.T. School methodology, proven effective over and over again in real-world hostage and terrorist situations.

When I give counterterrorism seminars to members of the American military and law enforcement, I strive to keep my message simple and to the point. The United States needs to face the fact that we are no different from Israel—we're an exponentially stronger and wealthier version of the Jewish state, to be sure, but fixed in the same terrorist crosshairs. And in my view, the Israeli model for domestic security is the only one we can follow—the only one that's ever been proven effective in the real world.

With its mandatory military service for all men and women, Israel is a nation of citizen-soldiers. Everyone is vigilant. If you live with terrorism on a daily basis, your reactions become subconscious, instinctive, visceral. You find yourself zeroing in on the tiniest clues and details. Often, you learn to discount what your eyes perceive.

You go with your gut—trusting something as vague as a disquieting feeling, mood, or odor.

A young, clean-cut, well-dressed Middle Eastern guy brushes past you in the street, smiling but with a faraway gaze, trailing a too-sweet wake of Drakkar Noir or Calvin Klein. A quarter-bottle of cologne signals nothing to most Americans—beyond questionable taste in personal grooming—but most Israelis will freeze on the sidewalk, minds racing with dark scenarios. . . . *Did I brush shoulders with a potential suicide bomber? Is the ill-fitting Polo shirt concealing a paunch—or a taped-up package of C-4? That cloying fragrance—is it a telltale sign that the would-be martyr stayed up all night bathing and anointing himself in cologne because he needs to smell pristine—primed for the journey to Paradise the instant his mission is accomplished?*

I am often asked how American domestic security compares to Israel's. I'm sorry to say that it doesn't compare favorably. The main difference is that the Israeli security system is built specifically to defend against acts of terrorism, a fact that even predates the nation's founding in 1948. American security remains a "feel good" system, with millions of dollars pumped into equipment that tends to sit around unused. I don't buy the Bush administration's explanation that there hasn't been another terrorist attack since 9/11 because we are better prepared. I think there hasn't been another major terrorist attack on American soil because the Arabs know that they don't need to attack the United States until *they're* ready. After all, eight years elapsed between the 1993 World Trade Center bombing and 9/11. There's a different conception of time in the Middle East. They will wait decades to strike again if need be. And right now there are more than enough Americans to shoot in Iraq.

Israel's security system is truly multilayered. It begins with the constant visibility of the Israel Defense Forces and the Yamam counterterrorism unit, and continues through the domestic police force; it is followed by the armed security guards patrolling at every bus station, hotel, school, and shopping mall. It's a holistic system that can completely mobilize itself within forty-eight hours—all the core skills of every man and woman in the entire, elaborate, overlapping network are designed specifically for counterterrorism.

Israel's security efforts are highly visible and ubiquitous. Soldiers on the streets bear rifles, uniformed police officers carry pistols, undercover agents on street corners, in malls, and on buses constantly scan for potential threats. You cannot walk into a restaurant without having your bag checked. Everybody is scrutinizing everybody else. That may sound like a kind of collective paranoia but it is the way the nation functions. Israel is a society that's been turned upside-down psychologically in order to survive and protect itself.

Police cars always cruise the streets with their blue lights flashing, even when they aren't en route to an emergency, because Israeli officials want the public to know that at any given time the police are nearby, ready to respond to a terror threat. However, it's not a case of the "boy who cried wolf." Israeli police do not drive with the *sirens* wailing. If the sirens of a police car suddenly go on, everyone knows that an act of violence has just occurred. Maybe it's an act of terror; maybe not. But when you hear sirens in Israel you immediately think, *Terrorist attack!* And it's a signal for people to start rallying.

The Israeli government regulates all security guards in Israel.

The average security guard is a twenty-two-year-old IDF discharge, paying his way through college after three years in the military. Every security guard in Israel is armed and has a minimum of forty hours at a counterterrorism school. The security guards at the Central Bus Station in Tel Aviv are ex-IDF servicemen armed with Uzis. That alone is a powerful visual deterrent. They are trained to shoot into crowds with pinpoint accuracy. Should a guard's gun jam, he is also trained in Krav Maga. Most important, he is trained in profiling and predicting suspicious behavior: someone whose clothes are mismatched; someone walking with zombielike tunnel vision, no peripheral glances, as if on a mission; someone who's pale, sweating, or stuttering; a vehicle parked in the wrong place too long. He's trained to listen for a certain type of Hebrew accent that doesn't sound like a Yemenite or Moroccan Jew—it sounds distinctly like a Palestinian speaking Hebrew.

If a bag is left unattended for a few minutes, he'll sound the alarm and evacuate the Central Bus Station. Compare that to *our* level of readiness. Even post-9/11, someone could leave an unattended bag on a bus in Los Angeles or New York and, odds are, no one would even notice, much less react, for hours.

Every school in Israel is surrounded by a security fence with gates at the entrance; at the gate sits a guard—typically, fresh from his three years of IDF service—with a handgun. In addition to being an expert marksman, the guard is also trained in evacuating the schoolchildren the moment he perceives an active terrorist threat. The neighborhood police department is frequently invited to the school to coordinate counterterrorist training with the guard and school staff, just the way we have fire drills in the United States. Every worst-case scenario is practiced and practiced, ad infinitum.

My company does private security for several Jewish private schools in Southern California, and I recently began teaching a school safety module based on the Israeli system. The first thing I did was spend three hours drilling the teachers and staff on how to run into a classroom, secure the children, and hide them from a potential killer. Technically, it's called "active-shooter training"—it's mandatory in Israel but how many teachers in this country are given the opportunity to learn it? I make them run drills until they are exhausted, showing them how to keep the kids from going into a state of panic even in a hostage situation. The goal is to make the children invisible. What a terrorist cannot see, he cannot shoot. In Israel, blood is never shed in vain. After the Ma'alot school massacre in 1974, drills were developed, teachers were trained with an eye toward their ability to protect the students, security fences were erected. Imagine the lives we could have saved in America if we had been similarly adaptable, if the lessons of the Columbine tragedy could have prevented the Amish school killings of 2006 or the rampage at Virginia Tech in 2007.

American domestic security has historically been based on an anticrime model and it has been very hard to switch to a counterterrorist model because, simply put, we've had very few terrorist acts on our soil, and none since 9/11. The Federal Bureau of Investigation was specifically designed to handle gangsters like John Dillinger, Pretty Boy Floyd, the bank robbers and gunslingers of the Depression. Today the FBI deals with white-collar crime and the remnants of the Mafia. Local police forces are trained to deal with armed robbers, murderers, rapists, drug dealers. As a matter of fact, drugs were the main focus of all levels of U.S. law enforcement pre-9/11. When cops weren't giving tickets, they were chasing dope.

The Israelis, on the other hand, aren't spending much manpower on domestic crime. As a consequence, drugs, prostitution, and gambling have become rampant in the poorer quarters of Israeli cities. Newspapers are filled with lurid stories of car bombings and drive-by assassinations among the Israeli Mafia crews, largely turf wars over gambling and drug territory. But per capita, crime remains a very small problem in Israeli life. There is organized crime and gambling but little street crime like muggings and rapes. The average Israeli, going out on the town in Tel Aviv or Jerusalem, doesn't worry about a robber or rapist; he worries about the café or the pizzeria being blown into a million pieces by a suicide bomber.

The main threat to the typical Israel's safety is an Arab terrorist. It may be harsh for Americans to face this reality, but an Arab—any Arab—is seen as a potential terrorist in Israel. Consequently, Israelis profile Arabs—at airports, at bus stations, at all roadside checkpoints leading into the country. I'm not interested in sugarcoating this reality. The security apparatus in Israel views the entire Arab populace as a threat because almost every terrorist act committed against Israel, with the exception of a tiny minority of German and Japanese radical groups, has been perpetrated by Arab men. That's who the Israeli government defense systems are geared toward. The military, police, airport security, private security, school guards—the entire network is designed to recognize and respond to the Arab threat.

Everyone knows that the security at Israeli airports and on airplanes is the best on earth. Every flight manifest is cross-checked with terrorist watch lists. Not only is there the visible deterrent of uniformed security guards checking every aspect of every flight, there are undercover security agents scanning, studying, and covertly interviewing potential threats before they board the planes. Oftentimes, covert agents are mixed in with the actual passengers standing in line, eavesdropping on conversations. All bags are screened, of course, but El Al, Israel's national airline, looks at the person *before* they look at the suitcase.

El Al security training is rigorous. The course to become a certified El Al security agent lasts several months and is followed by a stringent selection process that screens for a certain disciplined, unflappable personality type.

Each agent is trained in sophisticated psychological techniques. They will ask routine questions such as "Whom did you visit in Tel Aviv?" or "Did you eat in anyone's home?" The questions are not designed to elicit any kind of specific information, but rather to evaluate the passenger's body language, which determines whether the agent continues with more intense—even rude—questioning. The more passive the person becomes when they are asked a rude question, the more scrutiny they will come under. The more defensive a person becomes when asked a rude question, the more likely that he or she is telling the truth.

There's no set routine to the preflight interview; the questions change for every passenger, adding an element of surprise. The interview might only be two minutes long (an eternity compared to the rubber-stamping that usually occurs at U.S. airports), but the agents know precisely what to look for. Beyond the most obvious tics—difficulty maintaining eye contact, shallow breathing, excessive perspiration, answers that sound too rehearsed—many details of El Al's security screening procedures remain too classified for me to divulge here.

And while profiling is a critical component of the screening process, it's not limited to ethnicity by any means. Single women traveling alone are often tagged as "high-risk" passengers due to the possibility that they may be used in terrorism-by-proxy plots, the most famous of which occurred at Heathrow Airport on the morning of April 17, 1986, when El Al security agents found explosives hidden in the lining of a bag carried by Anne Mary Murphy, a pregnant Irishwoman who was booked on a flight to Tel Aviv. Murphy had been given the suitcase by her fiancé, a Jordanian named Nezar Hindawi, and was wholly unaware of its contents. (When the El Al supervisor asked her about the explosives, Murphy reportedly blurted out: "The bastard tried to kill me!") Hindawi had escorted her to Heathrow and instructed her not to mention his name since he knew full well that the Israeli security agents would interrogate her closely if they learned she was engaged to marry an Arab man. Nevertheless, after intensive questioning revealed someone else had paid for her ticket, the explosives were discovered. (Hindawi was captured and sentenced to forty-five years in a British prison.)

Near disasters like the Hindawi incident are one reason that, even in foreign airports like Heathrow, JFK, or LAX, El Al insists on maintaining its own stringent standards, which include putting all luggage through a decompression chamber with which to trigger hidden explosives.

There is a similar gulf between the two nations' sky marshal programs. American sky marshals tend to be men in three-piece suits, with a dead-give-away Marine Corps haircut and visible bulges in their jackets that indicate, at even a casual glance, that they are armed. On Israeli flights, the sky marshals are undercover. Young, fit, and hyperobservant, the Israeli may pass himself off as a tourist on his way to an ashram in India. Meanwhile, he's watching, covertly profiling every passenger, ready to effect a takedown even before someone can attempt to hijack the plane.

The American system is too high and tight; too much emphasis on weight lifting and not enough on thinking. In this country, we still haven't learned to develop the crucial human elements, from the sophisticated use of psychological profiling, to being able to blend into the environment.

Is American society ready to put in place the needed measures? We certainly have the money, and the mission has been clearly defined: to protect the homeland. Israel focuses the majority of its energy on reducing the collective risk to the nation. I firmly believe we can change the system in this country, if we have the political will to do so. But the public has not yet come around to the necessity of politically incorrect yet vitally important techniques such as profiling, nor are they necessarily willing to start showing up three hours ahead of their departure times to endure a vigorous psychological screening process based on the El Al model. But just think how much better they'd feel once the plane takes off. Meanwhile, the policy makers in the United States have yet to grasp that for all the millions being allocated for high-tech equipment like retinal scanners, the human brain, when properly trained, is still the best piece of security equipment out there.

TWENTY-FIVE

How can the United States improve its overall level of counterterrorism readiness? The answer to that question may depend, to an extraordinary degree, on policy. In Israel, the counterterrorism policies are far more detailed and institutionalized than they are here. In 1974, after waves of terrorist kidnappings of Israeli civilians and soldiers, the operational wing of the Israel Defense Forces issued a landmark order that formalized and codified the response of all counterterrorist units in the country in the event of a hostage crisis:

ISRAELI DOCTRINE AGAINST HOSTAGE-TAKING TERRORISTS

The Special Operations Units of the IDF and the Israel National Police will take over and eliminate *terrorists who perform such attacks.*

The operation must be executed as quickly as possible in order to thwart any achievements made by the terrorists specifically pertaining to surrendering to their demands.

Therefore, our main operational goal in the event of a terrorist-related hostage situation will be:

1. Save the lives of as many hostages as possible.
2. Kill the terrorist(s).

The U.S. policy has yet to be similarly defined. All too often, I find myself walking into a law enforcement agency and asking the captain in charge of a SWAT team, "Where's your rulebook on counterterrorism?"

"We don't have one," he'll respond.

In Duvdevan, and in every other Israeli counterterrorism unit, there's an actual book—a classified binder—that lays out the specific policies on every conceivable scenario.

In the United States, we have no fixed rules or policies on how to handle terrorists and active shooters such as the Virginia Tech gunman. Much of what I teach my American cops is completely counterintuitive for them. For example, if a terrorist takes cover in a crowd of civilians, you have to be trained to take him down with a pinpoint shot that avoids killing innocent bystanders. American police learn no such skill. When I teach them how to shoot into a crowd, American cops go bananas. Their jaws drop. *Holy shit!* they say. Because they've never even seen that attempted, let alone advocated as an effective policing strategy.

Under the Israeli system, we train with thousands of rounds of ammunition; we practice the same drill thousands of times, over and over, learning how to run into a crowd, using voice commands, and employing dynamic movement to manipulate our way through a mass of people in order to be able to identify active terrorist threats.

The average SWAT unit in the United States, especially in smaller cities, is a part-time team. That's one of the major holes in our response system toward lethal threats. When faced with a terrorist or active shooter, the most important predictor of success is the sheer number of hours the responding officers have logged preparing for that response. Shooting thousands of rounds is critical. Learning to shoot in teams, with two or more officers working in tandem, is something Israelis practice constantly. An American police officer shoots, on average, once every three to four months for his qualification. And that means shooting at a firing range, in a standing position, at a static target thirty feet in front of you. Two to the body, one to the head. That's *not* real-world response training.

In Israel, a typical cop or counterterrorism operator will fire his weapon up to twelve hours a day during training, constantly in motion, drilling in real-world scenarios.

Indeed, the most critical lesson I can teach is that *you have to take the fight to the terrorist.* I have to constantly remind my trainees, "Guys, you have to run *into* the threat." Attacking an active shooter is not easy; it goes against both human nature and common sense. But it's an essential skill in rapidly defusing a hostile situation with an absolute minimum of gunplay, far more effective than limiting your men to firing two rounds to the body and one to the head, then requiring every bullet to be accounted for in a post-shooting review. Israelis are trained to shoot until the target goes down and then to sprint over to the body and put one bullet in the head, just in case he has enough strength left to detonate whatever explosives may have been strapped to his body. Over and over I tell my classes, "You can't save people's lives unless you attack and *kill* the threat."

When I'm hired to train American police SWAT teams or military units, I do not try to impart anything that's classified; I've never taught a unit how to kidnap somebody the way we would in Duvdevan, for example. What I'm giving them is the general Israeli response methodology and the mind-set to be able to get to the threat as quickly as possible, so that more innocent people aren't killed. I don't waste their time teaching them how to hit a bull's-eye. They are already crack marksmen.

The problem I come across over and over when working with local cops is that they have learned one way of thinking about crisis intervention, and they haven't had the real-world experience to see how ineffective it is. Their police agencies are filled with millions of dollars of high-tech equipment—mobile command centers, staging vehicles, mammoth trucks loaded with state-of-the-art emergency response equipment. Usually, it's gathering dust in the back parking lot of the police station, never having been employed, waiting for the possibility of a terrorist attack. It's the best equipment in the world, equipment the officers have never been trained on and are likely never to use in their careers.

Granted, the average American cop has historically been unlikely to face an Islamic terrorist in his tour of duty. But how long before some terrorist straps on an explosive vest and boards a New York City subway train or a Chicago bus during rush hour? We can't stop every threat, of course, but we can *minimize* the risk. We need to constantly train our first-responders to be ready for the worst-case scenarios. All the high-tech equipment in the world won't stop a terrorist determined to drive a truck bomb into a crowded metropolitan area or to leave a Semtex-packed suitcase unattended in a shopping mall. But an armed and vigilant police presence, combined with bomb-sniffing dogs, profiling, and aggressive questioning of anyone acting suspiciously, along with a watchful, involved general public could make the difference between a lone dead terrorist lying on the stone floor of Grand Central Station and a catastrophic loss of life.

It's a matter of calculating lives *saved* versus lives *lost*. Americans look at things from a liability perspective rather than tabulating how many innocent lives were saved.

Ever since the infamous Rodney King incident, which sparked riots all over Los Angeles and other major cities, American law-enforcement agencies have been under a microscope in terms of civil liberties. There's no denying that many actions that save lives in Israel would be considered excessive use of force in United States, but we are in danger of turning our policemen into complacent watchdogs, unable to react in a timely fashion when lives are at risk. Required to wait for management to give them the go-ahead before they act, our rank-and-file police officers will never acquire the kind of judgment, reflexes, and instincts they need—and want—to learn to combat the threats of the twenty-first century. Over and over I see politics get in the way of real-world effectiveness.

It's very difficult—when I know what is achievable with the proper manpower, training, and political will—to sit and back and listen to people say we mustn't let America become another Israel. *What about our civil liberties?* they lament. The classic Israeli answer is this: Explain civil liberties to the parents of the dead kids.

Los Angeles 2007

I recognize that what I've written here may sound unduly harsh, pro-militaristic, even anti-Arab in places—but I am writing this book not as a propagandist but as a pragmatist. Do I want peace with the Palestinians? Of course. Do you think that the *vast* majority of Israelis don't want peace with the Palestinians?

Israel's greatest tragedy in my lifetime was the assassination of Yitzhak Rabin. Rabin was a towering figure, willing to extend his hand to the Arabs for peace. Yet he was murdered by an extremist—a fanatical, homicidal *Jewish* maniac—for his efforts.

Yitzhak Rabin was killed in November 1995, when I was an active warrior with the unit. I had gone to the kibbutz to visit Dror Schapiro and the Weiss brothers when the news broke that Rabin had been killed. I will never forget how distraught and sickened they looked. These were some of the hardest sons-of-bitches I ever met and some of them were bawling like little kids.

They kept saying things like:

"How? Why? Rabin was the *best*! Rabin was the *light*! He was *our* prime minister."

Soon I started seeing bumper stickers everywhere saying SHALOM, CHAVER—"Peace, Friend"—a phrase that President Bill Clinton made internationally famous when he delivered a moving eulogy at Rabin's funeral. The whole country was devastated, because they knew they'd lost the best chance for peace with security we would see in our lifetime.

So Israel soldiers on. They protect themselves as best they can. And they go back to that famous, defining speech of Moshe Dayan, uttered back in 1955:

> We cannot protect every water pipe from being blown up, nor every tree from being uprooted. Nor can we prevent the murder of the workers in the orchards, nor of families in their beds, but we *can exact a high price for our blood*, a price too high for the Arab community, the Arab army, the Arab governments to pay.

I lived by that philosophy every day in my service in the IDF, and I still live by it today. For all the sensational headlines about horrific terrorist attacks, it's incalculable how many would-be martyrs have been intercepted and neutralized by the quick thinking and relentless preparation of Israelis, both active military personnel and average civilians.

After the trauma of 9/11, I thought the collective American mentality might change. But here we are seven years later, still playing a pitiful game of catch-up, desperately cranking the wheel of the *Titanic* long after the iceberg's been sighted. My colleagues at IMS are dumbfounded by the state of America's domestic security. *Can you believe they're still making people take off their shoes at the airport?* they'll ask. *Why are they screening luggage more carefully than they screen people?* In Israel, they seek to inhabit the enemy's mind in order to predict what he'll do next week, whereas we have remained fixated on what his confederates did last year.

This security stratagem may have been perfected in recent years by Israel. But it's not inherently Zionist. It's not even new. Two thousand years ago Sun Tzu wrote his famous dictum: *To win without fighting is best.* In Israel, this doctrine of aggressive preemption has been internalized as a national credo. When the time for fighting ultimately comes, you must constantly adapt. Be as fluid as water, penetrating the cracks of the enemy's complacency. "Just as a military force has no constant formation, water has no constant shape," Sun Tzu writes in *The Art of War*. "The ability to gain victory by changing and adapting according to the opponent is called genius."

Acknowledgments

This book offers a portrait of *my* Israel: my personal journey through the IDF; my training and missions with the unit; experiences which I continue to hold very dear. I must stress that, as with all elite units, tactics, operating styles and leadership change over time. Units like mine must always remain adaptable, especially in the ever-shifting reality of the counterterrorism battle in the Middle East. The Unit has undergone a significant evolution, both tactically and operationally. In these pages, I have not attempted to represent how Duvdevan functions at the present time, merely how I experienced it in the mid-'90s, when I was fortunate enough to serve with my brotherhood of warriors—*lochemim* like Ilan, David, Inon, Udi, Amir, Elad, Eitan, Eliav. . . .

This book would not have been possible without the tireless efforts of numerous people. I owe an immense debt of gratitude to

Douglas Century, my coauthor and good friend; Daniel Halpern and Lee Boudreaux, my editors at Ecco; Richard Abate, my literary agent at Endeavor; Steve Katz, my manager; and Gilad Millo, of the Consulate General of Israel in Los Angeles. Finally, I want to thank my mother, Myra. Back when I was a teenager, getting bounced from school and sent away to learn some discipline, I could not appreciate what a difficult time she had in raising me. I also could never have dreamed that I would one day join her in sharing a passion for the writing life.